THE GAY TRIVIA
QUIZ BOOK

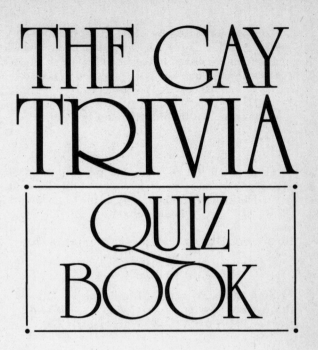

THE GAY TRIVIA QUIZ BOOK

by James Aaron

ARBOR HOUSE
New York

Library of Congress Cataloging in Publication Data

Aaron, James.
The gay trivia quiz book.

1. Homosexuality, Male—Miscellanea.   I. Title.
HQ76.A225   1985   306.7′662   84-24512
ISBN 0-87795-638-3 (alk. paper)

For Mark and Jon, of course

Many thanks to Lois and Susan

Contents

THE GAY TRIVIA
QUIZ BOOK

PERSONALITIES

From W. H. Auden, Rupert Brooke, and Carl Van Vechten to Harvey Fierstein, Lorenz Hart, and Doric Wilson, some of the most colorful and interesting people have been—*Oh, my God, it can't be true*—gay.

In the last few decades gay people have become more open about their homosexuality, but some of the most intriguing gay personalities still remain closeted because of societal pressure. Here, some gossip tidbits about well-known gay authors, cooks, actors, and others are revealed.

1. What famous gay poet, after paying homage to W. H. Auden, knelt and kissed Auden's trouser cuffs before leaving?

    A) Rod McKuen
    B) Allen Ginsberg
    C) Percy Bysshe Shelly
    D) None of the above

2. Carl Van Vechten, black photographer, writer, dandy, and true renaissance man of Harlem during the 1920s and

1930s, wrote books that were elegant and, yes, just a little gay. A famous line in one of his books is, "A thing of beauty is a boy forever." What is the title of the book?

A) *The Blind Bow-Boy*
B) *The Boy from Over the Tracks*
C) *The Randy-Dandy*
D) *Randy Andy*

3. Henry Lord Darnley, the father of a gay king of Scotland and England, was murdered at age twenty-two while with a boy whom he was engaging in sex. What was the king's name?

A) King Henry II
B) King George V
C) King James I
D) King Charles IV

4. What actress, famous for her "drop dead" line, was torn between her many affairs with women and her love for men?

A) Mary Martin
B) Marilyn Monroe
C) Judy Holliday
D) Tallulah Bankhead

5. What actress reportedly once found comfort in an affair with a female drama coach?

A) Marilyn Monroe
B) Janet Gaynor
C) Doris Day
D) Ava Gardner

6. Sergei Diaghilev, whose Ballet Russe first performed some of the most important ballets of the twentieth century, made one of the following his lover, then his choreographer. Who was he?

A) Leonide Massine
B) Serge Lifar
C) Vaslav Nijinsky
D) Rudolf Nureyev

7. This well-known playwright writes for "alternative theater," for gay audiences, and is known for his consistently frank treatment of the gay experience. His plays include *Forever After, A Perfect Relationship, The West Side Gang*. Who is he?

A) Edward Albee
B) Doric Wilson
C) Lanford Wilson
D) Harvey Fierstein

8. This gay porno legend was born in Los Angeles in 1946. He has survived the business and still remains one of that industry's main attractions. Who is he?

A) John Holmes
B) Jack Wrangler
C) Casey Donovan
D) Tim Kramer

9. What king of France abandoned himself completely to homosexuality during the last years of his reign, surrounding himself with handsome young men, throwing wild orgies, dressing up in drag, and indulging in S & M?

A) Louis XV
B) Louis XIV
C) Henri III
D) Georges I

10. What Russian painter, whose works include *Portrait of My Father* (1939) and *Hide and Seek* (1941), had numerous homosexual lovers, including surrealist painter René Crevel and the American writer Charles Henri Ford?

A) Vladimir Romanski
B) Pavel Tchelitchew
C) Alexander Igorovich
D) None of the above

11. For three thousand gold pieces, this Roman emperor lured the powerful Roman statesman Hirtius to his bed and returned the favor by having Hirtius murdered once he became emperor, just to make sure his secret would be safe. Who was he?

A) Augustus Caesar
B) Agathon
C) Octavius
D) Antinius

12. Radclyffe Hall's *The Well of Loneliness* was the first undisguised lesbian novel. Like all of this author's novels, it was dedicated to "the three of us." One person in the dedication was Hall's lover, Veronica Batten, a woman more than twenty years her senior. Who was the other person?

A) Lady Una Troubridge, another lover of Hall who dropped dead in the midst of a quarrel with

Veronica Batten. To assuage her guilt, Hall forever dedicated her books "to the three of us."
B) Lady Allison Hamilton, the third party in a life-
long *ménage à trois* between the author and
Veronica Batten.
C) It wasn't a person at all, but "Minnie," the pet
poodle Hall and Veronica Batten had with them
throughout twelve years of their relationship.
D) Hall's mother, who knew about and accepted
Hall's love affair with Veronica Batten—quite unusual for the time—and lived with the couple
until she died.

13. Before he started writing music with Oscar Hammer-
stein II, Richard Rodgers wrote music for the lyrics of a man
whose homosexuality was a carefully guarded secret until
thirty-five years after his death. Who was the lyricist?

A) Lorenz Hart
B) Cole Porter
C) Alfonzo Raffaelo
D) None of the above

14. This woman feared writing about lesbianism, anticipat-
ing a diminution of the value of her work. Nevertheless, she
did write a novel entitled *Mrs. Stevens Hears the Mermaids
Singing* (1965), which features a homosexual woman who is,
in the author's words, "neither pitiable nor disgusting, without sentimentality." Who is the author?

A) Mary Renault
B) Erica Jong
C) Elizabeth Bowen
D) May Sarton

15. This silent film star's sexuality has been widely debated, but the consensus is that he was gay, as is indicated in his journals, where he writes about making love to a man. What is his name?

    A) Tom Mix
    B) Rudolph Valentino
    C) Buster Keaton
    D) None of the above

16. Said to be America's first great actress, this woman, born in 1816, began as an opera singer, but lost her voice and turned to drama. Her roles included Romeo and Hamlet, and her affairs with women are well known and documented. Who is she?

    A) Fanny Kemble
    B) Eliza Cook
    C) Matilda Hays
    D) Charlotte Cushman

17. Although this writer dressed as a man, wrote novels under a male pseudonym, and is known to have had several lesbian affairs, lesbianism is never portrayed in her novels. Who is she?

    A) Charlotte Laughton
    B) George Sand
    C) Amandine Aurore Lucie Dupin
    D) None of the above

18. What writer was born in New Orleans and was as well known for his life-style as his writing?

A) Truman Capote
B) Rex Reed
C) James Baldwin
D) Gore Vidal

19. Greta Garbo's life has been filled with gay men, but the gay man who discovered her and became her mentor and friend was a spectacular failure at MGM as a director. Who was he?

A) Frank Capra. Though he had many successes elsewhere, every film he made at MGM flopped.
B) John Huston
C) Mauritz Stiller
D) Robert Stewart

20. In 1976, this famous rock star confided to *Playboy* that he was bisexual. Who is he?

A) Elton John
B) Mick Jagger
C) Rod Stewart
D) David Bowie

21. True or false? Sal Mineo produced a revival of *Fortune and Men's Eyes*, starred in a West Coast production of James Kirkwood's *P.S. Your Cat Is Dead*, and supposedly "turned queer" after the auto wreck that took James Dean's life, his costar in *Rebel without a Cause*.

22. This man, whose collection of Greek art forms the core of the collection at the Boston Museum of Fine Arts and New

York's Metropolitan Museum of Art, wrote the three-volume *Defense of Uranian Love*, an apologia for pederasty, as embodied in the Greek art that he loved. He also wrote *A Tale of Pausanian Love* about homosexuality at Oxford. Who was he?

A) Gunnar Myrdal
B) Gerard Manley Hopkins
C) Terence Rattigan
D) Edward Perry Warren

23. Traces of amyl nitrate ("poppers") were reportedly discovered in this actor's body. Some even speculate that he died of a popper-induced heart attack. Who is he?

A) Sal Mineo
B) Burt Ward, who played Robin in the "Batman" TV series
C) Paul Lynde of "Hollywood Squares" fame
D) Melvyn Douglas, who made one of his last appearances in *Being There*

24. This former inspector general of the United States originally trained men under Frederick the Great for his Prussian army, but lost favor when it was discovered that he took "indecent liberties" with some of his students. What is his name?

A) Baron Alfred von Mageburg
B) Baron Friedrich von Steuben
C) Count Wilhelm von Lichtenstein
D) Sir William Hamilton-Carter

25. The nineteenth-century poet and philosopher Ralph Waldo Emerson refers in his journals to his crush on a classmate at Harvard, an infatuation considered now to be a classic example of adolescent homosexuality. Though later in life Emerson tried desperately to remove all references to his "love," enough remains to give us a clear picture of who he was. What was his name?

A) Martin Gaye
B) Gerald Walker
C) Dudley Milton
D) Dudley Doright

26. This poet died when he was only twenty-seven, but after his death he was canonized by the British, as much for his poetry as for the loss of one of Britain's truly beautiful young men, who was also a soldier and a man of valor. His poetry was clearly homoerotic, and in the 1920s, actress Tallulah Bankhead claimed to have read love letters he wrote to another young man. Who is this poet?

A) Walter Pater
B) Rupert Brooke
C) Goldsworthy Dickinson
D) Charles Warren-Stoddard

27. What two British kings with the name of Richard were gay?

A) Richard II and Richard the Lion-Hearted
B) Richard I and Richard II
C) Richard IV and Richard I
D) None of the above. There were no British kings named Richard who are known to have been gay.

28. What Swedish queen was known to be lesbian?

A) Oona
B) Anna
C) Abba
D) Christina

29. The author of *Lyndon: An Oral Biography* has also written several books dealing with homosexuality. Who is he?

A) Seymour Hersh
B) Allen Drury
C) Merle Miller
D) David S. Broder

30. This well-known poet married, even though he was so infatuated with a seventeen-year-old boy named Arthur Rimbaud that he brought him into his home to live with both him and his wife, where they openly continued their homosexual affair. Who was he?

A) Paul Verlaine
B) Algernon Swinburne
C) Walt Whitman
D) W. H. Auden

31. Though known for his flamboyant homosexual affairs, Oscar Wilde married and fathered two sons. What was his wife's name?

A) Constance Sayre
B) Henrietta Martin
C) Constance Lloyd
D) Erika Mann

32. What were the names of Oscar Wilde's sons?

    A) Bruce and Gerald
    B) Vivyan and Bruce
    C) Gerald and Oscar, Jr.
    D) Cyril and Vivyan

33. Erika Mann, daughter of Nobel Prize–winning author Thomas Mann, married a famous homosexual poet so that she could get a British passport. Who was he?

    A) Yukio Mishima
    B) Algernon Swinburne
    C) W. H. Auden
    D) Lord Byron

34. What U.N. secretary general, generally thought to have been gay, had a Manhattan plaza named after him?

    A) Kurt Walheim
    B) Dag Hammarskjöld
    C) Shimon Peres
    D) Menaheim Meir

35. The British playwright Joe Orton once said he had "high hopes of dying in my prime," and shortly thereafter the man who wrote *Loot* was killed by his lover. How was he killed?

    A) He was electrocuted when an electric cattle prod was shoved up his anus.
    B) He was strangled to death with the rope his lover had, moments before, used to tie him up in an S & M session of sex.
    C) He was beaten to death with a hammer
    D) He was slashed to ribbons with a power saw.

2

LIFE-STYLES

As with any group of people, there are certain aspects of gays' lives—some positive, some negative—that distinguish them from others.

Here, answers to questions about sports groups, meeting places, gay resorts, and more will give you an overall perspective on the gay life-style.

36. On which of the following dates did Margaret M. Heckler, Secretary of Health and Human Services, announce in Washington, D.C., that "the probable cause of AIDS has been found"?

> A) April 23, 1984
> B) May 2, 1984
> C) April 19, 1984
> D) None of the above

37. The name of the virus that the government and researchers believe to be the cause of AIDS is:

A) LAV
B) HTLV-2
C) HTLV-3
D) A and C, but not B

38. In 1984, an athletic event sponsored by Front Runners NY and the New York *Native* drew thousands of gay men and women and was sanctioned by the Metropolitan Athletic Congress and the New York City Department of Parks and Recreation. What was the name of this event?

A) The Gay Pride Run
B) The Gay Swim for MS
C) The New York Gay Marathon
D) The Nellie Parade

39. What famous football player became the first professional athlete to tell the world that he is a homosexual?

A) Earl Campbell
B) Joe Namath
C) David Kopay
D) None of the above

40. What was the above player's position?

A) Running back
B) Halfback
C) Quarterback
D) Receiver

41. Which team did he play on?

A) San Francisco Forty-Niners
B) Detroit Lions
C) Washington Redskins
D) All of the above

42. In the heart of New York's gay community, there is a bookstore that attracts customers not only for its books, but for its "back room," which houses New York's largest selection of all-male videotapes. What is the name of the store?

A) Christopher Street Book Shop
B) The Erotic Male Book Shop
C) The Sixty-Niner's Bookstore
D) Pink Flamingos Books

43. In the 1970s a famous New York City bathhouse burned, killing nine people. What is the name of this bathhouse?

A) Luxor Baths
B) St. Mark's Bath
C) Club Bath
D) Everard Bath

44. Ad Memorium released a record, a twelve-inch version of "Menergy/Take You Home/Megamedley," whose profits were donated to the Gay Men's Health Crisis in the fight against AIDS. In 1982, the artist died of AIDS. Who was it?

A) Patrick Cowley
B) Sly Funk
C) Garrick Wayne
D) Zoli

45. Which well-known public official said, in reference to AIDS, "This epidemic will be with us for the rest of our lives"?

    A) President Ronald Reagan
    B) Secretary of Health and Human Services Margaret Heckler
    C) Dr. James Curran, director of the AIDS Task Force, Centers for Disease Control
    D) None of the above

46. True or false? Nearly a hundred thousand of the one million carriers of hepatitis B in the United States are gay men.

47. True or false? There is a National Gay Alcoholics Anonymous with its central office in New York.

48. What is the medical term for warts that appear on the penis and anus?

    A) Condyloma acuminatum
    B) Multiple verricula
    C) Anuswartis
    D) None of the above

49. What is the drug, widely used at the discos in the 1970s, and during sex, that is applied to a handkerchief, inhaled by sucking on the cloth, and gives an explosive rush?

    A) Butyl nitrite
    B) Amyl nitrate
    C) Ethyl chloride
    D) Ethyl alcohol

50. Fire Island has been known for decades as a summer mecca for gays and straights seeking sun, fun, and dancing along the seashore. Specifically, the areas of Fire Island that attract the most gays are:

    A) The Pines
    B) Kismet
    C) Point O' Woods
    D) Cherry Grove

51. Amyl nitrate and butyl nitrite—popular among gays for the "rush" they give—are commonly referred to as "poppers" because:

    A) When inhaled, the drugs "pop" the blood vessels.
    B) Pharmaceutical amyl nitrate, which comes in glass ampules and is usually encased in a special gauze matrix, makes a popping sound when the ampules are snapped by the fingers.
    C) When inhaled, cells in the brain literally "pop."
    D) None of the above

52. Which of these groups had "cross-dressers," the forerunner of today's transvestites?

    A) Aztec shamans
    B) Persian catamites
    C) American Indians
    D) All of the above

53. True or false? Transsexual males do not perceive themselves as homosexual when they have sex with men, even before surgery, because psychologically and spiritually they feel like women.

54. Which of the following tennis player's career was ruined when it was discovered that he was homosexual?

    A) Bill Tilden
    B) Bobby Riggs
    C) Bjorn Borg
    D) None of the above

55. The Village People, a rock band best known for the hit songs "YMCA," and "Macho Man," got its start in gay discos and became one of the hottest bands of the late seventies. How many people were a part of the original band?

    A) Six
    B) Five
    C) Four
    D) Seven

56. True or false? In an orgy room at the baths, it is considered rude to observe and not participate.

57. True or false? Most baths, except for the Club Bath chain, do not require membership fees or admission charges—only a deposit on the room.

58. What is the most common slang for back-room "25¢ movie booths," which show pornographic homosexual films?

    A) Blow-holes
    B) Glory-holes
    C) Show-holes
    D) None of the above

59. At the Mine Shaft, the most notoriously decadent gay club in New York, a gay man will not be admitted if he:

    A) Wears cologne
    B) Wears a striped shirt
    C) Wears designer clothes
    D) All of the above

60. True or false? Downstairs at the Mine Shaft, one of the star attractions is a tub in which people can lie down and be urinated on.

61. The slang term for the above is called:

    A) Yellow rain
    B) Golden showers
    C) Water sports
    D) B and C, but not A

62. At the Pines in Fire Island, there is a section of open sand dunes just off the beach where gay men can go at any time of the day or night to have sex. This section is known as:

    A) Fairy's Forest
    B) MacArthur's Park
    C) Stretch Beach
    D) The Meat Rack

63. True or false? The fastest way of getting to the Pines on Fire Island is by car.

64. True or false? One of Fire Island's major attractions is its inexpensive accommodations. Summer house rentals and motel accommodations are reasonable and accessible to gays living in and around New York.

65. Rita Mae Brown, best known for her books *Rubyfruit Jungle* and the recent *Sudden Death,* had a real-life love affair with a famous woman tennis star. Her name is:

    A) Tracey Austin
    B) Billie Jean King
    C) Martina Navratilova
    D) None of the above

66. Gays who solicit or engage in sex in public rest rooms call these places:

    A) John-johns
    B) Tearooms
    C) Throat lounges
    D) All of the above

67. "Cock rings" are metal, leather, or rubber rings worn by gays during sex. The reason they are worn is:

    A) To maintain an erection by closing off the flow of blood into the penis
    B) To enlarge the appearance of the testicles, which is often considered quite sexy
    C) To give the male a more "butch" look
    D) All of the above

68.   Cock rings come in a variety of styles and designs, most of which either look like metal rings or small leather dog collars. But many have an additional feature, which is used to spread the testicles apart. This is called:

    A) A nutcracker
    B) Ball spreader
    C) Nut clamp
    D) None of the above

69.   True or false? In most gay movie theaters in metropolitan areas, it is considered inappropriate to have sex while the movie is going on, and management usually encourages patrons interested in such encounters to leave.

70.   What was the name of the young man who filed the $200 million-plus palimony suit against Liberace, claiming that he had provided sexual favors to the singer?

    A) Scott Thorngood
    B) Scott Thornson
    C) Scott Thorson
    D) Scott Thompson

3

HISTORY

Believe it or not, gay history started before Stonewall. In fact, there are indications that homosexuality has been around since Adam and, well, Eve.

Although the role of homosexuality in history is not as well charted as it might be, it *is* a history to be valued nonetheless. See how much you know about our gay forefathers.

71. True or false? New York State's first governor was a transvestite. In fact, he often appeared in public in drag.

72. The first reported trial for an alleged homosexual offense took place during the reign of:

    A) King Charles I
    B) King Edward II
    C) King Henry VIII
    D) Queen Victoria

73. Oscar Wilde, author of, among other books, *The Picture of Dorian Gray,* was put on trial for his homosexual exploits. How many times did this happen?

A) Two
B) Six
C) Four
D) Three

74. Which of the following legislation has most influenced modern Western attitudes toward homosexuality?

A) Novel 77, issued by the emperor Justinian in A.D. 538
B) Novel 141, issued by Justinian in A.D. 544
C) Code 1120, issued by the Council of Napolous in the Holy Land
D) The imperial legislation of Christian Rome promulgated in A.D. 390 by the emperors Theodosius I, Valentinian II, and Arcadius.

75. True or false? Plato, Aristotle, and Euripides were all gay.

76. True or false? Pederasty was an intrinsic and accepted part of the Greek military and educational systems.

77. When was the first organization to lobby for changes in public opinion and laws on homosexuality formed?

A) 1721
B) 1897
C) 1947
D) 1919

78. What was the name of the first organization of lesbians in the United States

> A) Daughters of the Republic
> B) Sisterhood
> C) Daughters of Bilitis
> D) The Toklas-Stein Foundation

79. When was this organization formed?

> A) 1927
> B) 1955
> C) 1956
> D) 1947

80. *One* magazine was published by One, Inc., an organization formed to protect the rights of homosexuals. It was distributed through the mails until October 1954, before it was:

> A) Halted because One, Inc., had disbanded after a tremendous amount of infighting
> B) Pulled from the mail by the postmaster of Los Angeles
> C) Stopped from further publication because right-wing groups such as the John Birch Society had destroyed its printing presses in a riot
> D) Discontinued due to a lack of funding

81. What was the stereotypical profession for gay men during the 1800s in America?

A) Haberdasher
B) Barber
C) Theater manager
D) Variety store clerk

82. What king was forced to witness the beheading of his gay lover, which had been ordered by his father?

A) King George II
B) Alexander the Great
C) Frederick the Great
D) King Juan Carlos I

83. What term was used during the 1950s as a euphemism for *homosexual* by those who wanted to fight the stereotype that homosexuals were obsessed with sex?

A) Gay, which is still in use today
B) Queer, preferred by neoconservative homosexual men because it highlights the fact that they are different
C) Queen
D) Homophile

84. The last half of this century saw the publication of a book that was considered a landmark because, for the first time, it presented homosexuals as a minority deprived of rights and status by a prejudiced society. What was the name of the book?

A) *The Politics of Homosexuality* by Toby Marotta
B) *The Homosexual in America* by Donald Webster Cory

C) *The Oscar Wilde Handbook* by Bruce Phallus
D) *The Homosexual Matrix* by C. A. Tripp

85. On which date did eight police officers set out and fail to close the Stonewall Inn, a gay bar in Greenwich Village, thanks to the patrons, who fought back? (The ensuing riot marks the birth of the Gay Liberation Movement.)

A) June 27, 1969
B) July 21, 1968
C) June 23, 1969
D) August 2, 1970

86. What is considered one of the earliest, if not *the* earliest, magazines to be published dealing with topics of interest to lesbians?

A) *Lesbos*
B) *The Dyke Review*
C) *Lesbian Inc.*
D) *Alternative*

87. When did the American Psychiatric Association vote to remove homosexuality from its list of mental disorders?

A) April 1974
B) June 1973
C) December 1971
D) June 1975

88. What is the name of the first national organization in America established to promote homosexuality?

A) Vice-Versa
B) Mattachine Foundation
C) One, Inc.
D) Quaker Emergency Committee

89. What was the Quaker Emergency Committee?

A) A committee formed by homosexual Quakers to aid other gays in legal or financial trouble
B) A group formed in New York by Quakers, dedicated to assisting homosexuals in conflict with the law
C) An emergency committee formed immediately after World War II by the Quaker Oats Company to fight prejudice toward blacks, Jews, Catholics, and gays
D) None of the above

90. In Los Angeles right after World War II, a gay black man founded an organization to provide gay social services and to involve gays and straights of both sexes and all races in concerns of social harmony. This is probably the earliest group to unite gays with other oppressed minorities, a pattern that characterized the gay liberation decade of the 70s. What was the name of this organization?

A) The Knights of the Clock
B) The Bachelor Foundation
C) Forever Bachelors
D) Prince of Peace Foundation

91. What was the name of the first gay university organization founded in America?

A) Student Gay Action Committee
B) Student League of Gays
C) The University of ——— Homophile League
D) Student Homophile League

92. At what university was it founded?

A) New York University
B) Harvard
C) Columbia
D) UCLA

93. When was the organization founded?

A) April 1967
B) September 1965
C) February 1968
D) May 1969

94. Who was the first gay to speak as a gay on radio?

A) Allen Ginsberg, poet
B) Kate Millett, author
C) Randolphe Wicker, businessman
D) Christopher Isherwood, author

95. Don Slater, one of the founders of One, Inc., a gay organization, and Harold Call, founder of Mattachine/San Francisco, were the first gays to appear as such in what straight magazine?

A) *Look*
B) *Newsweek*
C) *U.S. News & World Report*
D) *Life*

96. What year did Call and Slater appear in the magazine?

    A) 1964
    B) 1967
    C) 1969
    D) 1966

97. What New York mayor used to frequent the gay Sunset Club in drag?

    A) Fiorello La Guardia
    B) Jimmy Walker
    C) John Lindsay
    D) Ed Koch

98. By what decade had the word *gay* become the self-descriptive phrase of choice among homosexuals?

    A) The fifties
    B) The twenties
    C) The sixties
    D) The thirties

99. Anarchist Emma Goldman wrote and lectured on the implication of lesbian/feminist perspectives for American society up until:

    A) The thirties
    B) The twenties
    C) The forties
    D) The fifties

100. Because of his reportedly uncommon mannerisms,

Vice-President William Almon Wheeler, while serving as senator from New York, was nicknamed

A) "Aunt Wheeler"
B) "Miss Thing"
C) "Girlfriend"
D) "Sister Wheeler"

101. When was the first television appearance in America by a gay on behalf of gays?

A) October 1962
B) December 1965
C) June 1969
D) April 1964

102. It is well known that Eleanor Roosevelt had a very close relationship with another woman for many years. Even during the first lady's years at the White House, this woman lived in the Roosevelts' private quarters. What was her name?

A) Kay Summersby Morgan
B) Judith Exener
C) Lorena Hickock
D) Gladys Johnson

103. What were the names of the two homosexual spies from the British Foreign Office who defected to Russia in 1951, setting in motion one of England's most vicious witch-hunts?

A) Allan Leeds and John Meredith
B) Donald Maclean and Alan Turning
C) Donald Maclean and Guy Burgess
D) Alan Maxwell and Gary Sullivan

104. In June 1947, the earliest known publication in the United States for lesbians was published. What was the pseudonym of the woman who started it?

A) "Geri Allen"
B) "Vicky Robinson"
C) "Lisa Ben"
D) "Roberta Moss"

105. In what year was the first Gay Liberation Day observed?

A) 1970
B) 1969
C) 1971
D) 1972

106. A seventeenth-century English clergyman who said, "Buggery is no sin" was forced to resign his church post because:

A) He was caught stealing from the parishioners' offerings.
B) He seduced and made love to six eight-year-old children
C) He had sex with three parishioners and a mare
D) He forced his wife into a lesbian affair.

107. To whom are the following words attributed: "All of them that love not tobacco and boys are fooles"?

A) William Shakespeare
B) Jonathan Swift
C) D. H. Lawrence
D) Christopher Marlowe

108. The Sultan Saladin of Crusader times was asked by King Richard the Lion-Hearted which he preferred, girls or boys. Saladin's response was:

    A) "Girls. It's kind of tough to make a baby with a boy."
    B) "Neither. Animals please me most."
    C) "Whatever's available."
    D) "Girls? Allah forbid!"

109. *Pedicon* is the Latin word for a male who "exercises his member" in another man's anus. What is a *cinede?*

    A) A man who receives the male "exercising his member" in his anus
    B) A man who likes to have sex with young boys
    C) A man who doesn't like to be touched by other men
    D) A man whose penis is so large that he cannot have sex with another human being

110. Curio the Elder made the following remark about a very famous Roman: he is "the husband of all woman, and the wife of all husbands." To whom was he referring?

    A) Petronius
    B) Caesar
    C) Emperor Galba
    D) Seutonius

111. "A boy of twice ten is fit for a king!" is a line from what great work?

A) *The Marquise of O*
B) *The Thousand and One Nights*
C) *Manchild in the Promised Land*
D) *Giovanni's Room*

112. Who said the following? "At least 37 percent of the male population [of the United States] has some homosexual experience between the beginning of adolescence and old age."

A) Oscar Wilde
B) Tennessee Williams
C) Alfred Kinsey
D) Gore Vidal

113. According to the Roman Athenaeus, what people "take more pleasure in pederastia than any other nation, to such a degree that amongst them it is no rarity to find a man lying between two minions"?

A) Celts of France
B) Tyrrhenians of Italy
C) Sodmorians of Chicago
D) Rimmorians of Poland

4

FILM

Hollywood is known to be the home of the stars. It's also a place where homosexuals have made a formidable contribution to modern culture and entertainment. Unfortunately, when it comes to homosexuality, Hollywood is probably one of the most closeted communities—rumors about major stars who have been paid major bucks to keep their gayness very private abound. It's a fact: gay stars spell box-office losers.

Gay people are featured in films, both in those made with big studio money and those done by the more modest independents; but more often than not the portrait is not a flattering one. In the last few years, this situation seems to have improved, but Hollywood still has a long way to go. Find out just how much you know about gays in films.

114. In which 1895 film did two men dance a waltz together?

43

A) *A Woman*
B) *Let's Fall in Love*
C) *The Gay Brothers*
D) *Don't Step on My Toes, Tina*

115. Which Alfred Hitchcock film was advertised as the "most excitement-filled love story ever told" and focused on the dubious deeds of two gay men?

A) *Strangers on a Train*
B) *Rope*
C) *The Lodger*
D) *The Man Who Knew Too Much*

116. In a scene cut from a 1962 movie the two lead actresses were found guilty of having had "sinful sexual knowledge of one another." What was the movie and who were the actresses?

A) *After the Foxes,* Julie Christie and Elizabeth Taylor
B) *Persona,* Liv Ullman and Bibi Anderrson
C) *West Side Story,* Rita Moreno and Natalie Wood
D) *The Children's Hour,* Audrey Hepburn and Shirley MacLaine

117. What actress played a lesbian madam in Edward Dmytryk's screen version of Nelson Algren's *A Walk on the Wild Side?*

A) Julie Andrews
B) Tippi Hedren
C) Barbara Stanwyck
D) Debbie Reynolds

118. In a 1963 film, Shelley Winters tells Lee Grant that "whores are a dime a dozen, but a good bookkeeper is hard to find." In this film, Winters kisses Grant, which earned the film the description of "lesbian letch" in a *Variety* review. What is the name of this film?

    A) *The Balcony*
    B) *The Poseidon Adventure*
    C) *A Place in the Sun*
    D) *Orca*

119. Who costarred with Ryan O'Neal in *Partners,* a 1983 flick about a straight cop who "goes gay" to help find a murderer who has killed several gay men?

    A) Al Pacino
    B) Harvey Fierstein
    C) John Hurt
    D) Perry King

120. Cliff Robertson played a presidential candidate accused of homosexuality in a Franklin Schaffner film. What was the name of the film?

    A) *Bedtime for Bonzo*
    B) *Advise and Consent*
    C) *The Best Man*
    D) *King Rat*

121. In a 1973 movie actor Edward Fox kills a gay man he meets in a bathhouse. What is the film and who directed it?

    A) *Ordinary People,* Robert Redford
    B) *Sunday, Bloody Sunday,* John Schlesinger
    C) *The Day of the Jackal,* Fred Zinneman
    D) *The Big Sky,* Howard Hawks

122. In the film version of Thomas Mann's *Death in Venice,* who played the role of Aschenbach, the middle-aged man who becomes obsessed by the young boy Tadzio?

    A) Hardy Kruger
    B) Dirk Bogarde
    C) Michael York
    D) Richard Chamberlain

123. William Friedkin's *Cruising* caused an uproar in the gay community because of its myopic view of gay life. Who played the straight cop who comes to realize that he is gay during the course of his investigation of a gay murder?

    A) Tom Selleck
    B) Peter Fonda
    C) Al Pacino
    D) Dustin Hoffman

124. In a film starring Jane Fonda, Anita Pallenberg was featured as the Black Queen and John Phillip Law as a Gay Angel. What was the film's title, the director, and the year the film was made?

    A) *Won Ton Ton,* Michael Winner, 1976
    B) *X, Y & Zee,* Brian Hutton, 1971
    C) *The Third Sex,* Frank Winterstein, 1959
    D) *Barbarella,* Roger Vadim, 1968

125. George Sanders had a wild time cavorting about as a San Francisco drag queen in what movie?

    A) *The Magic Christian*
    B) *The Eiger Sanction*

C) *The Kremlin Letter*
D) *The Anita Bryant Story*

126. James Bond movies are not known for being highly populated by gay characters. In which Bond flick are two gay lovers part of the scenery, and what makes them special?

A) *Goldfinger.* The lovers each have their pinkies dyed gold.
B) *Never Say Never Again.* The lovers become presidents of the United States.
C) *Diamonds Are Forever.* Killing people is the lovers' specialty.
D) *Dr. No.* Rejecting Russian vodka at the port of entry is the job both characters hold.

127. Cliff Gorman plays an effeminate gay man in George Cukor's *Justine.* How does Gorman's character meet his filmic death?

A) He is electrocuted in a Jacuzzi at a gay bath.
B) A hatpin is inserted in his neck.
C) He falls from the top of the Empire State Building.
D) He is murdered by his mother.

128. In what 1972 film does Tony Perkins play a gay man with suicidal tendencies?

A) *Cabaret*
B) *Lenny*
C) *A Clockwork Orange*
D) *Play It as It Lays*

129. George Lazenby plays a gay senator in a 1979 Peter Bogdanovich film. What is the film?

    A) *Rocky*
    B) *Taxi Driver*
    C) *Saint Jack*
    D) *Paper Moon*

130. In what 1959 movie is a young man "cured" of his homosexuality by his mother?

    A) *The Third Sex*
    B) *Marty*
    C) *On the Waterfront*
    D) *Ben Hur*

131. In *Rachel, Rachel* Estelle Parsons plays a psalm-singing lesbian spinster. Who directed *Rachel, Rachel?*

    A) Montgomery Clift
    B) Paul Newman
    C) Estelle Parsons
    D) Norman Lear

132. In Ken Russell's *Tommy*, a character named Uncle Ernie is shown reading what newspaper?

    A) *The Advocate*
    B) *New York Native*
    C) *Blueboy*
    D) *Gay News*

133. In a 1978 movie starring Richard Gere, Bruce French plays a gay jeweler who refuses to talk to or see his homo-phobic father. What is the film and who directed it?

A) *Nashville,* Robert Altman
B) *American Gigolo,* Paul Schrader
C) *Bloodbrothers,* Robert Mulligan
D) *Rocky II,* Sylvester Stallone

134. What movie, like the play it was based on, takes place during a party for a gay man celebrating his birthday?

A) *Mame*
B) *The Boys in the Band*
C) *Where the Boys Are*
D) *Lover Come Back to Me*

135. What film directed by John Schlesinger has at its cen-ter a homosexual doctor, a heterosexual career woman, and a bisexual artist?

A) *Darling*
B) *Julia*
C) *Sunday, Bloody Sunday*
D) *Marathon Man*

136. In a 1975 film, Al Pacino robs a bank, in part, because he needs money to pay for his lover's sex change operation. What is the name of the film?

A) *The Family Way*
B) *Dog Day Afternoon*
C) *A Different Story*
D) *Meet Me in St. Louis, Louisa*

137. In what 1960 film does a transvestite character predict that by the year 2000 everyone will be homosexual?

    A) *The Days of Wine and Roses*
    B) *Imitation of Life*
    C) *Tea and Sympathy*
    D) *La Dolce Vita*

138. What is unusual about the two lesbian lovers in Robert Altman's *A Perfect Couple?*

    A) They are portrayed as happy and well adjusted— a family.
    B) Each of the women is over seven feet tall.
    C) They wear dresses.
    D) Making love with men is their favorite hobby.

139. In what 1976 movie does a transvestite character named Lindy tell another character who makes fun of Lindy's apparent lack of masculinity, "Honey, I'm more man than you'll ever *be* and more woman than you'll ever get"?

    A) *Next Stop, Greenwich Village*
    B) *Car Wash*
    C) *Taxi Driver*
    D) *The Turning Point*

140. In a 1974 film, Alan Bates plays a gay teacher who makes himself and everyone around him miserable. What is the name of the film?

    A) *The Loved Ones*
    B) *The Virgin Spring*
    C) *Butley*
    D) *Deliverance*

141. In what movie did Herbert Ross direct Michael Caine as the gay husband to Maggie Smith's movie star?

A) *The Broadway Melody*
B) *Sunset Boulevard*
C) *Mahogany*
D) *California Suite*

142. Paul McCrane plays Montgomery, an openly gay student at the High School of the Performing Arts, in which of the following movies?

A) *Fame*
B) *A Star Is Born*
C) *The Rose*
D) *Hair*

143. Ads for a 1960 movie featured Sal Mineo screaming, "They used me—like a woman!" What was the name of the film?

A) *The Christine Jorgensen Story*
B) *To Sir, with Love*
C) *Exodus*
D) *Funny Lady*

144. Who delivered the following line in the 1972 film *They Only Kill Their Masters:* "Isn't a pregnant lesbian a contradiction in terms?"

A) Barbra Streisand
B) Bette Davis
C) Shelley Winters
D) June Allyson

145. In what 1980 film did Richard Gere play a male prostitute who "didn't do fags"?

    A) *On the Waterfront Redux*
    B) *Annie*
    C) *Rocky II*
    D) *American Gigolo*

146. Celebrated entertainer and pianist Liberace played a "flaming homosexual" casket salesman in *The Loved One*. In the same film, who played Mr. Joyboy?

    A) Rod Steiger
    B) Jonathan Winters
    C) Roddy McDowell
    D) Paul Lynde

5

RELIGION

For many, gays and religion just don't mix. There are even those who would banish homosexuals from their places of worship. But religion is an integral part of—and exerts a profound influence on—many gays' lives. And when it comes to the history of religion, as in secular history, homosexuality plays a key role. Test your knowledge about gays and religion.

147. True or false? The word *homosexual* does not appear once in either the Old Testament or the New Testament.

148. True or false? Lesbianism is generally ignored in the Bible.

149. The Metropolitan Community Church is by far the largest gay Christian church in the United States, with MCC ministries not only in most large U.S. cities, but throughout the world. When was this church founded?

    A) October 6, 1968
    B) December 25, 1972
    C) July 1, 1969
    D) May 2, 1959

150. The founder of the Metropolitan Community Church is the Rev. Troy D. Perry, a minister ostracized by his own church because of his homosexuality, who felt that he had a call to establish the MCC as a place whose doors would be open to all of God's children without distinction or discrimination. Rev. Perry's story is told in his autobiography, entitled:

    A) *Thy Rod and Thy Staff*
    B) *Faith, Fellowship, and Gaiety*
    C) *The Lord Is My Shepherd and He Knows I'm Gay*
    D) *Memoirs of a Gay Christian*

151. In 1973, the Faith, Fellowship, and Order Commission was established at the General Conference of the Metropolitan Community Church, at which more than sixty congregations gathered. From this came, in 1976, the first major report culled from the grass roots of the church—women and men, lay people and clergy—from the United States, Great Britain, Canada, and Australia. What did this report explain?

    A) The MCC's theology
    B) The MCC's finances and five-year plan for expansion

C) The MCC's political and religious philosophy
D) None of the above

152. What was the title of this report?

A) *The FFO Commission Report on Homosexuality and the MCC*
B) *The MCC Today, Tomorrow, and for Eternity*
C) *United We Stand: The MCC Report*
D) *In Unity: The Gay Christian*

153. Homosexuals of another religion were inspired by the MCC's efforts. These homosexuals formed a gay-oriented Jewish synagogue called:

A) Beth Israel
B) Chaim Chaham Chadashim
C) Boychick Haddas
D) None of the above

154. True or false? Though Protestant denominations of the sixteenth century differed on many issues, homosexuality was not one of them.

155. Where is the earliest explicit mention of homosexuality in the Bible?

A) Leviticus
B) Genesis
C) Exodus
D) The Book of Job

156. True or false? The antihomosexual aspects of the biblical story of Lot's daughters were probably inserted long after the original Scriptures were written as a part of an anti-Greek campaign in Palestine when Judaism was under great stress from outside influences, especially those of Greece.

157. True or false? None of the biblical condemnations of homosexuality refers to Sodom.

158. True or false? Jesus is not quoted anywhere in the Bible as saying anything about homosexuality.

159. What born-again Christian disco queen said at a recent concert—and to a predominantly gay audience—"I love you all, but remember, God made Adam and Eve, not Adam and Steve"?

    A) Viola Mills
    B) Diana Ross
    C) Donna Summer
    D) Irene Cara

160. What famous conservative evangelist said that he believes homosexuality is caused by the lack of a masculine image in the child's family? (For example, when the father has left home and the son adopts the traits of his mother.)

    A) Jimmy Swaggart
    B) Oral Roberts
    C) Jerry Falwell
    D) Pat Robertson

161. Which of the following twelfth-century Jewish poets, apparently disregarding Judaism's stand against homosexuality, wrote gay erotic verse, which was actually love poetry to various youths?

    A) Moshe-ibn Ezra
    B) Ibn Sahl
    C) Ibn Ghayyath
    D) All of the above

162. During the Middle Ages, "passionate friendship" was the subject matter of much of the writing of the period, as well as almost all of the love poetry (including poetry with homosexual themes). True or false? Most of the authors were priests.

163. Which of these biblical figures had intense love relations with persons of their own gender in the Old Testament?

    A) Saul
    B) Ruth
    C) David
    D) All of the above

164. Where does the passage "Your love was wonderful to me, passing the love of women" appear in the Bible?

    A) The Book of Job
    B) Leviticus
    C) 2 Samuel
    D) Matthew

165. According to the most conservative biblical interpretations, how many references are there in the Bible to gay people?

A) Twenty-one
B) Seven
C) Nine
D) Twelve

166. What was the name of the first ecumenical ("general") council to rule on homosexual acts?

A) Latern III
B) Latern II
C) The Philistine Council of Saints
D) Our Blessed Virgin Council of 1710

167. True or false? In the fourteenth century, adultery incurred more severe penalties in church law than did sodomy.

168. Saint Aelred of Rievaulx, who wrote eloquently of homosexual love in a Christian context in his treatises *The Mirror of Charity* and *On Spiritual Friendship,* himself fell in love with two men. They were:

A) Monks in his order
B) Clergy in his parish
C) Altar boys in the cathedral, who, under his guidance, eventually became priests
D) Hired hands who helped him oversee his church-owned estate in France

169. A devout Catholic, this king went to mass every day for most of his life, was the driving force behind the third Crusade, remained in the Holy Land long after the other leaders had returned to Europe, favored the church in his lands, and kept close spiritual company with the church's leaders. However, when he was a young man, he fell in love with Philip, king of France, and eventually became his lover. Who was he?

A) Richard I
B) George II
C) Henry IV
D) Richard the Lion-Hearted

170. Baudri of Bourgueil (1046–1130), abbot of the French Benedictine monastery of Saint Peter and archbishop of Dol, was also known for his:

A) Blatantly open affair with the parishioners within his archdiocese
B) Openly homoerotic poetry
C) Being driven from office twice due to charges of sodomy
D) None of the above

171. What controversial book won the 1980 American Book Award for history and created a stir among religious groups for its reassessment of biblical interpretations of homosexuality?

A) *Homosexuality—from the Beginning of the Christian Era to the Nineteenth Century*
B) *Christianity, Homosexuality and the Bible: A New Interpretation*
C) *Christianity, Social Tolerance and Homosexuality*
D) *The Christian Gay: A Redefinition*

172. What San Francisco church affiliated with the Methodist church, became for a time the center of gay activities in the San Francisco area?

    A) Glide Memorial Church
    B) The Church of Interdenomination
    C) The Fellowship of Brothers
    D) The United Christian Church

173. In what year did the Episcopal House of Bishops come out against the ordination of practicing homosexuals?

    A) 1972
    B) 1978
    C) 1981
    D) 1975

174. In what year did the general assembly of the United Presbyterian Church reject the report of a special task force stating that practicing homosexuals could and should be ordained to the ministry or allowed to hold key offices in the church?

    A) 1978
    B) 1979
    C) 1980
    D) 1974

175. Despite the above official stands against homosexuality, there have been several homosexual support groups of various denominations. Dignity is an organization for gay ——; and Integrity is an organization for gay ———.

    A) Episcopalians, Catholics

B) Presbyterians, Episcopalians
C) Unitarians, Catholics
D) Catholics, Episcopalians

176. In Genesis 1:28, the story of ——— has been taken to justify the condemnation of contraception, masturbation, and homosexuality, because none of these results in procreation.

A) Abel
B) Haddas
C) Jonah
D) Onan

177. *Forum* is the monthly newsletter of:

A) *Penthouse*
B) Integrity
C) Dignity
D) Lutherans Concerned for Gay People

178. The Committee of Friends is:

A) An organization involved in promoting the discussion of bisexuality among Quakers
B) A committee formed by Gay Lutherans
C) A committee formed for the promotion of interests and ministries of the Unitarian church
D) None of the above

179. True or false? The Baptist religion still doesn't have a gay caucus.

180.   True or false? The National Gay Task Force has not yet formed a religious committee, believing instead that the various denominational organizations will handle that aspect of homosexual life.

181.   Evangelicals Concerned is:

    A) A national task force of gay and straight evangelicals concerned about the lack of preparation for dealing realistically with homosexuality in the evangelical community

    B) A national task force concerned about the implications of the gospel in the lives of gay men and women

    C) An organization of concerned hard-line evangelicals determined to combat proponents of more lenient attitudes toward homosexuality, which they still consider sinful and a sickness

    D) A and B, but not C

6

MUSIC

Throughout history, sexuality—and homosexuality—have played a vital role in the music world, in the lives of composers and performers, as well as in their lyrics.

So, what about Michael Jackson, Elton John, and George Handel? Read on and find out.

182. What popular rock group released a song entitled "Little Caesar" in 1982 with the lyrics, "I've been called a lot of names/some of them obscene . . . back in the days of funny funny/they called me queer"?

    A) Culture Club
    B) The Rolling Stones
    C) Blondie
    D) Abba

183. What tormented composer detested his homosexuality, was terrified that he would be "discovered," was at one time passionately in love with his sister's son, "Bob," and yet ended up marrying a nymphomaniac *woman* nine years his junior?

A) Shubert
B) Bach
C) Vivaldi
D) Tchaikovsky

184. Reynaldo Hahn, one of Paris's most popular composers at the turn of the century, was a key member of a club of well-known homosexuals in Paris at the time, a group that included Sergei Diaghilev, Lucien Daudet, and Jean Cocteau. Hahn is also noted for being the first lover of:

A) Marcel Proust
B) André Gide
C) René Crevel
D) Hart Crane

185. There has been a great deal of speculation about Michael Jackson's sexual preferences, but one indication may be a song he wrote, "Muscles," that deals with the love of men's bodies. On which Diana Ross album does this song appear?

A) *Pieces of Ice*
B) *The Boss*
C) *Diana*
D) *Silk Electric*

186. What song, performed by Culture Club, supposedly deals with lead singer Boy George's broken homosexual love affair with his former roommate?

A) "Karma Chameleon"
B) "Do You Really Want to Hurt Me?"
C) "I'll Tumble 4 Ya"
D) None of the above

187. What renowned female blues singer sang "Foolish Man Blues," several lines of which go, "There's two things got me puzzled, there's two things I don't understand;/That's a mannish-acting woman, and a skippin', twistin' woman-actin' man"?

A) Josephine Baker
B) Bessie Smith
C) Gladys Ferguson
D) Billie Holliday

188. According to Ned Rorem in his *Paris Diaries*, this composer was once known to chase pretty Arab boys through the back streets of French North Africa and had as his lover the famous French baritone Pierre Bernac. His name is Francis:

A) Sinatra
B) Vines
C) Poulenc
D) Holmes

189. True or false? David Bowie, whom we already know has admitted to his bisexuality in *Playboy,* at one time used to perform mock blow jobs on members of his audience during concerts.

190. What famous female rock singer is well known for her sexual exploits with women?

A) Grace Slick
B) Joan Jett
C) Janis Joplin
D) Patti Smith

191. True or false? George Frederick Handel, the famous German composer born in 1685, was not only gay, but a transvestite.

192. What well-known composer wrote the definitive depression opera *The Cradle Will Rock*?

A) Bertolt Brecht
B) Thomas Weill
C) Marc Blitzstein
D) None of the above

193. This same composer was working on an opera about Sacco and Vanzetti when, in 1968, in Fort-de-France, he was murdered by:

A) His lover, who placed the composer's head in a grand piano and slammed the lid down repeatedly until he died.
B) His former wife, who, upon arriving at her villa, where her ex-husband had gone to discuss business, found him in bed with her present husband (she also shot the husband)
C) A young, gay hustler

D) A washed-up French movie director with whom
    the composer had been having an affair

194. This woman was considered responsible for the harpsi-
chord's return to popularity during the twentieth century.
She was the most renowned keyboard artist of ancient music
on this instrument and, though married, was known throughout the music world as a lesbian. She was:

A) Wanda Rogers
B) Wanda Landowska
C) Wanda de Fellatio
D) Wanda Williwonka

195. This composer, born and raised in America, introduced the tone cluster, played with the arm or the fist, and
wrote pieces that were meant to be played directly on piano
strings. He is well known as an admirer of the music of
Charles Ives, but is even more well known for his imprison-
ment for sodomy, which briefly halted his career. He is:

A) Henry Cowell
B) Henry Lithgow
C) Aaron Copland
D) Leonard Bernstein

196. Elton John, best known for such hits as "Bennie and
the Jets," "Tommy," and the recent smash "I Guess That's
Why They Call It the Blues," admitted at the height of his
career that he was bisexual. Where did he first talk about this
publicly?

A) *People*
B) "The Tonight Show"
C) *Playboy*
D) *Rolling Stone*

197.   David Bowie has written about lesbians in the army, a queen bitch, in which a man "dresses like a queen but . . . can kick like a mule," all of which have homosexual overtones. Which song from his most recent album, *Let's Dance,* contains the same implications?

A) "Modern Love"
B) "China Girl"
C) "Unconditional Love"
D) "Without You"

198.   True or false? "Tainted Love," by the group Soft Cell, is a song about lost homosexual love.

199.   What famous composer of the nineteenth century, when asked if he was homosexual, replied, "No, no, my dear, I am a pederast"?

A) Henri Busser
B) Camille Saint-Saëns
C) Percy Grainger
D) None of the above

200.   What famous drag queen, best known for her screen appearances, has also released an album?

A) Alice Phallus

B) Clitorius Leachman
C) Divine
D) Hot Chocolate

201. The name of the above drag queen's album is:

A) *Hot Rod*
B) *Jungle Jezebel*
C) *Dolls and Dildos*
D) *It's Raining Men*

7

THE PRINTED WORD

From ancient Greek poets to Maugham, Auden, and Vidal, homosexual writers have always exercised a powerful influence in the literary world. Because their works are often only subliminally homosexual, the public tolerates and even applauds writers whose lives and works run counter to what they generally accept.

Writers who deal more directly with the topic of homosexuality have a tougher time gaining readership and acceptance, but even they have managed to make their voices heard.

See how much you know about gay writers and their writing.

202.   It's clear from many of Carson McCullers's novels that she had a special sensitivity to the feeling of loneliness. Why?

      A) She had a lesbian love affair, which ended in tragedy.

B) She was continually searching for the woman she loved who had left her.

C) She was married to homosexual Reeves Mc-Cullers, who eventually killed himself.

D) She had a love affair with a composer who was also her husband's lover.

203.   In her first novel, *The Hotel* (1928), Elizabeth Bowen writes about:

A) The friendship between a young woman and a middle-aged widow

B) The friendship between a young man, his homosexual lover, and his wife

C) The interrelationships of a group of women, all living in a hotel, who share sex as well as friendship

D) A hotel in which all the guests are allowed to live out their sexual fantasies

204.   In *Si le grain ne meurt* André Gide describes climaxing five times in one night with Muhammed, a boy introduced to him by Oscar Wilde. One of the following men publicly expressed his skepticism about the veracity of this story. Who was it?

A) Scott Fitzgerald

B) Somerset Maugham

C) W. H. Auden

D) Norman Mailer

205.   Best-selling author Harold Robbins wrote a novel in which the hero is bisexual. The title of this novel is:

A) *The Lonely Lady*
B) *Memories of Another Day*
C) *Dreams Die First*
D) *79 Park Avenue*

206. True or false? In his research for the above novel, Robbins experimented with bisexuality to get inside his character and see what it was like.

207. We all know that Somerset Maugham, author of *Of Human Bondage,* among other books, was gay. But two of the closest people to Maugham were also gay. Who were they?

A) Oscar Wilde and Yves St. Laurent
B) Alan Searle and Bernard Berenson
C) Gerald Haxton and Robin Maugham
D) Countee Cullen and John Reed

208. Norman Douglas was one of the most original writers of the 1920s. His famous novel *South Wind* (1917) is set on an island called Nepenthe, which is inhabited by an extraordinary group of eccentrics, seen through the eyes of an English bishop. Part of the novel recounts:

A) How Douglas came to a similar island with his lover, where the lover was accidentally killed
B) How Douglas, in his research, fell in love with another man and lived happily ever after on a similar island for the rest of his life
C) How Douglas made up his mind to leave his wife and settle on a similar island and openly lead a gay life without fear of reprisal
D) How Douglas lost his lover on a similar island to another man

209. Anglo-Irish-German-Danish poet, novelist, mythographer, and critic Robert Graves (born in London in 1895) consistently maintains a macho stance in all of his works, but in his early years, Graves wrote a play about homosexuality entitled:

    A) *But It Still Goes On*
    B) *The Dandy*
    C) *The Nancy-Boy*
    D) *Bottoms Up*

210. True or false? W. H. Auden once wrote a poem about fellatio.

211. In 1964, what critically acclaimed writer wrote a now-famous essay on "camp," in which she said "homosexuals, by and large, constitute the vanguard—and the most articulate audience—of Camp"?

    A) Joan Didion
    B) Susan Sontag
    C) Margaret Atwood
    D) Elizabeth Hardwick

212. William S. Burroughs, author of, among other books, *Naked Lunch*, wrote a novel called *Cities of the Red Night*, published in 1981. Some of the characters in this novel were borrowed from Burroughs's previous books, among them the homosexual:

    A) Clem Snide the Private Asshole
    B) Countess de Gulpa and de Vile
    C) Half-Hanged Kelley
    D) Blum & Krup

213. Somerset Maugham lived for many years with his secretary-lover Gerald Haxton in a villa in the south of France, where Maugham courted many a friend, including renowned homosexuals Jean Cocteau and Noel Coward. What was the name of the villa?

> A) Villa Maugham
> B) Villa Mauresque
> C) Villa Cather
> D) Dube de Pointepesse

214. One of America's most distinguished living composers, who won the Pulitzer Prize for composition and has been called "the world's greatest composer of art songs" by *Time* magazine, is almost as well known for his diaries, the first volume of which was published to critical acclaim in 1966 and deals extensively with his homosexuality. Who is he?

> A) Marvin Hamlisch
> B) Elliot Carter
> C) Aaron Copland
> D) Ned Rorem

215. The above composer/author now lives in New York City and Nantucket. Where was he raised?

> A) Chicago
> B) Philadelphia
> C) Ceylon
> D) Aruba

216. Rita Mae Brown's novel about lesbianism, *Rubyfruit Jungle*, was a surprise underground best-seller and is now a classic. What is the title of Brown's first book?

A) *Six of One*
B) *Southern Discomfort*
C) *The Hand That Cradles the Rock*
D) *Rubyfruit River*

217. In her follow-up to the hugely successful *Fear of Flying*, Erica Jong's heroine, Isadora Wing, has a lesbian love affair. What is the name of this novel?

A) *Fanny*
B) *How to Save Your Own Life*
C) *Sisters*
D) *Fear of Crashing*

218. In the above novel, what is the name of the woman Isadora Wing has an affair with?

A) Charlotte Cooke
B) Katherine Allison-Jones
C) Rosanna Howard
D) Cindy Bullough

219. In this same novel, Isadora Wing's lover has problems reaching an orgasm. How is this finally achieved?

A) Isadora straps on a dildo and proceeds to rape her.
B) Her lover masturbates with a Dom Perignon champagne bottle.
C) Her lover uses a green plastic vibrator from Japan.
D) Her lover uses a shower massager.

220. In 1956, numerous novels dealing with homosexuality were published, among them *The Judgment of Paris* by Gore Vidal, James Baldwin's *Giovanni's Room*, and:

  A) *Compulsion* by Meyer Levin
  B) *From Here to Eternity* by James Jones
  C) *The Naked and the Dead* by Norman Mailer
  D) *Another Country* by James Baldwin

221. Patricia Nell Warren's *The Front Runner*, published in 1974, was instantly popular among gays and may well be the perennial work on male homosexual behavior. The novel is told in the first person, and the speaker is Harlan Brown, track coach at a college where:

  A) The founder and president is aware of and has accepted Brown's homosexuality
  B) Billy Sive, a runner seeking asylum from the University of Oregon, falls in love with Brown
  C) Brown's wife ultimately reveals that she, too, is gay and has an affair with the women's swimming team coach
  D) None of the above

222. Laura Z. Hobson, author of the novel *Gentlemen's Agreement* (later made into a movie starring Gregory Peck), wrote a novel in 1975 that grew out of her personal experience with a gay son. The novel was entitled:

  A) *Over and Above*
  B) *The Tenth Month*
  C) *The Other Father*
  D) *Consenting Adult*

223. In 1979, a novel about a clique of homosexually oriented officers and students at West Point was published. What was the name of this novel and its author?

A) *The Cardinal Sins* by Andrew Greeley
B) *The Lords of Discipline* by Pat Conroy
C) *Sins of the Fathers* by Susan Howatch
D) *Dress Grey* by Lucian Truscott IV

224. *Dancer from the Dance* by Andrew Holleran is probably one of the best-known and best-received novels about gay life published in recent times. Critics applauded Holleran for his haunting portrayal of one gay man's obsessional search for love. What was this character's name?

A) John
B) David
C) Malone
D) Frankie

225. True or false? Joseph Hansen, who has written several mystery novels featuring a homosexual private eye named David Brandsetter and a critically acclaimed novel entitled *A Smile in His Lifetime*, whose hero is homosexual, has himself been married for over forty years.

226. Besides being a novelist, Joseph Hansen is also a poet and:

A) An English professor at UCLA
B) The founder of the pioneering homosexual journal *Tangents*
C) The heir to the Fort Howard Paper Company fortune.
D) The man who helped William S. Burroughs kick his heroin habit

227. Edmund White's most recent work is the novel *A Boy's Own Story*, about a boy who yearns to express his forbidden sexuality as he comes of age. The first chapter of the novel originally appeared as "First Love" in a magazine, and then in another book. What are the names of the magazine and book?

A) *Stroke* magazine and *The Christopher Street Reader*

B) *Christopher Street* magazine and *The Best Gay Fiction 1980*

C) *Christopher Street* magazine and *Aphrodisiac: Fiction from Christopher Street*

D) *Manstyle* and *The O'Henry Awards*

228. What famous novelist said, "It is almost worse to be a woman than to be a fag"?

A) Truman Capote

B) Somerset Maugham

C) Gore Vidal

D) Oscar Wilde

229. Who wrote, "I'm an alcoholic. I'm a drug addict. I'm a homosexual. I'm a genius"?

A) Gore Vidal

B) Andrew Holleran

C) Somerset Maugham

D) Truman Capote

230. Two years after World War II, four important novels about homosexuality that reflected the war's influence were published. One of these was:

A) *The End of My Life* by Vance Bourjailly
B) *Some Came Running* by James Jones
C) *The Young Lions* by Irwin Shaw
D) *Gentlemen, I Address You* by Kay Boyle

231. The best-selling novel of the year in 1959 featured a homosexual relationship and became the author's best-known work. Name the book and the author.

A) *Koptic Court* by Herbert Kastle
B) *The Immortal* by Walter Ross
C) *Forever Amber* by Kathleen Windsor
D) *Advise and Consent* by Allen Drury

232. In 1976, a man named G. B. Edwards died, leaving among his personal papers a novel that was subsequently published and hailed as a lost masterpiece of English fiction. The last half dealt with homosexuality. What is the book's title?

A) *The Book of Ebenezer Le Page*
B) *A Most Foul Introduction*
C) *The Guernsey Chronicles*
D) *The Word's Light*

8

THEATER

Gays have long played an important role in the theater, and in recent years gay theater has actually meant big "box office" for the straight Broadway theatergoing audience.

See how much you know about the significant contributions gay people have made to the theater.

233. Actor Richard Gere starred in the Broadway production of a play about two gay men imprisoned during World War II. What was the name of the play, and who was the playwright?

A) *Mame,* Jerry Herman
B) *Bandits,* Harvey Fierstein
C) *Intermezzo,* Liz Smith
D) *Bent,* Martin Sherman

234. A 1915 play features a major homosexual character for the first time in the history of the theater. What was the name of the play and who was the playwright?

A) *Queen Bee*, Liana van Homer
B) *Edward II*, Christopher Marlowe
C) *Cleopatra in Nightland*, William Shakespeare
D) *Lord Bane's Foul*, Poulenc Satie

235. Three of playwright Harvey Fierstein's plays were combined to form one play that runs some four hours in length. It won the 1983 Tony Award for Best Play. What is the name of the play and who was the first actor to play the lead role?

A) *Equus*, Richard Burton
B) *The Fifth of July*, Christopher Reeve
C) *Torch Song Trilogy*, Harvey Fierstein
D) *International Stud*, Julio Iglesias

236. In what fourteenth-century play are there lewd puns about Cain's behavior with Abel, the devil, and his "boye" Garcio?

A) *You Only Kill the Things You Love*
B) *Paradise Revisited*
C) *Abel Was I*
D) *The Killing of Abel*

237. Playwright Jane Chambers was told, "Nobody's going to buy a movie script about lesbians." Taking this advice to heart, Chambers successfully changed the movie to a play. What was the name of the ill-fated screenplay/successful stage play?

A) *A Late Snow*
B) *Last Summer at Bluefish Cove*
C) *Gertrude Stein, Gertrude Stein*
D) *To Sara with Love*

238. John Wilmot, the earl of Rochester, wrote a farce published posthumously in Amsterdam in 1660. The farce has been described by William M. Hoffman, author of *Gay Plays: The First Collection*, as "a wonderful obscene gay vision." What is the name of Wilmot's farce?

    A) *Sodom: Or, the Quintessence of Debauchery*
    B) *The Glory of Gommorah*
    C) *For a Shepherd I'd Spare My Rod*
    D) *The Purple-Helmeted Warrior of Love*

239. Jerry Herman, Arthur Laurents, and Harvey Fierstein collaborated on a musical that had first been a highly successful movie and stage play. What is the name of the musical and what two actors played the gay lovers who are at the center of the musical's plot in the original Broadway production?

    A) *Baby,* Quentin Crisp and Charles Nelson Reilly
    B) *La Cage Aux Folles,* Gene Barry and George Hearn
    C) *Any Night in Greenwich Village,* Tommy Tune and Boy George
    D) *Your Own Thing,* Al Pacino and Joe Namath

240. What famous actress, using the pseudonym Jane Mast, wrote *The Drag,* billed as a "homosexual comedy in three acts"?

    A) Bette Davis
    B) Jane Fonda
    C) Mae West
    D) Donna Reed

241. Of the following playwrights, who has *not* written a play featuring a gay setting or a lead character who is gay?

    A) Oscar Wilde
    B) Harvey Fierstein
    C) Robert Patrick
    D) Lanford Wilson

242. There are numerous references to homosexuality in Shakespeare's plays. Which of the following does *not* make an overt reference to homosexuality?

    A) *Troilus and Cressida*
    B) *As You Like It*
    C) *The Tempest*
    D) *Twelfth Night*

243. Three plays comprise Harvey Fierstein's *Torch Song Trilogy*. What are they?

    A) *Boy Meets Boy, Nights on West Street,* and *Widows and Drag Queens First*
    B) *Latenight Laments, Castro Street Blues,* and *Friday Night at a Gay Bar*
    C) *International Stud, Fugue in a Nursery,* and *Widows and Children First*
    D) *Animals, The Glory Hole,* and *To Master, with Love*

244. Which of the following plays does *not* have a gay character?

A) *A Chorus Line*
B) *T-Shirts*
C) *Betrayal*
D) *A Taste of Honey*

245. Gay playwright Joe Orton was murdered by his lover of fifteen years in August of 1967. Which of the following plays is Joe Orton best known for?

A) *A Taste of Honey*
B) *Entertaining Mr. Sloane*
C) *Up the Down Staircase*
D) *Staircase*

246. Which of the following plays was not written by gay playwright Doric Wilson?

A) *Forever After*
B) *A Perfect Relationship*
C) *On Golden Pond*
D) *The West Side Gang*

247. *But It Still Goes On* is a play about homosexuality by a writer who is best known for his poetry and literary criticism. Who is the playwright?

A) Rupert Brooke
B) Tennessee Williams
C) Robert Graves
D) W. H. Auden

248. Playwright Terence McNally wrote a black comedy set in a gay bathhouse. What is the name of the play?

A) *The Continental Baths*
B) *A Streetcar Named Desire*
C) *Divine Madness*
D) *The Ritz*

249. Which of the following Tennessee Williams plays does *not* have or make reference to a gay character?

A) *Cat on a Hot Tin Roof*
B) *A Streetcar Named Desire*
C) *The Glass Menagerie*
D) *Night of the Iguana*

250. Which of the following plays by Lillian Hellman revolves around lesbianism?

A) *The Children's Hour*
B) *The Little Foxes*
C) *Come Back, Little Sheba*
D) *Watch on the Rhine*

251. Which of the following plays is set in a prison and contains explicit depictions of homosexuality as well as underlying homosexual themes?

A) *Glass Houses*
B) *Fortune and Men's Eyes*
C) *Equus*
D) *Tea and Sympathy*

252. Who is the playwright of *In the Fairy Garden*, a farce about two homosexuals who find themselves amidst a beautiful garden and a murder or two in the company of a not-so-nice fairy?

A) David Rabe
B) Robert Patrick
C) Patrick Dennis
D) Harry Kondoleon

253. Lanford Wilson, one of the most respected playwrights of the 1970s and 1980s, won the Pulitzer Prize for *Talley's Folly.* Which of his plays is about the Talley family, with a particular emphasis on Ken Talley, a homosexual who has trouble reacclimating to small-town life after coming home paralyzed from Vietnam?

A) *The Fifth of July*
B) *Balm in Gilead*
C) *The Hot L Baltimore*
D) *Home Free*

9

LINGO

Gay. Faggot. Butch. Dyke. All of these words, and many more, are part of gay lingo. But what exactly *is* gay lingo? It is the language coined by gay people to describe certain events, actions, etc., which the rest of the population may not understand. Gay lingo is a dialect. Gay lingo is a way for gay people to distinguish themselves from other groups, to show that they are proud enough to develop a special language.

Go ahead. Test your knowledge of gayspeak.

254. Which of the following is *not* a synonym for homosexual?

    A) Gay
    B) Faggot
    C) Lesbian
    D) Straight

255. If someone says that his gay male friend is a "rice queen," what does he mean?

A) That his friend only eats rice
B) That his friend prefers his romantic partners to be Oriental
C) That his friend is on a sushi diet
D) That his friend is afraid of Oriental men

256. Which of the following is *not* a synonym for lesbian?

A) Dyke
B) Diesel-dyke
C) Lesbo
D) Boy crazy

257. AIDS is the acronym for a deadly disease that has taken a particularly heavy toll on the gay community. What do the letters in AIDS stand for?

A) Anti-Intercourse Deficiency Syndrome
B) Acquired Immune Deficiency Syndrome
C) Alternating Immune Defense Syndrome
D) Anti-Inference Destructive Syndrome

258. You are a partner in a gay male couple. Your lover's parents are over for a Sunday dinner. During dinner your lover, in a weak moment, calls you "Miss Thing." How does your lover explain to your parents what "Miss Thing" means?

A) He coyly tells them to look it up in the dictionary.
B) He acts out what "Miss Thing" means.
C) He tells them that he calls you "Miss Thing" when he thinks you are putting on false airs or overplaying a situation.
D) He doesn't.

259.   A homophobe is a person who:

    A) Hates or is fearful of homosexuals
    B) Is scared of being homosexual
    C) Talks like a homosexual
    D) Is a first-year law student at the Moral Majority School of Law

260.   NAMBLA is the acronym for a highly controversial group in the gay community. What do the letters in NAMBLA stand for?

    A) North American Man/Boy Love Association
    B) New American Master/Boss Love Association
    C) North American Mixed Bisexual Love Affiliation
    D) New American Mother/Boy Love Association

261.   A "fag hag" is:

    A) A cranky gay man or woman
    B) A gay man who likes to spend all his free time with heterosexual women
    C) A straight woman who likes to hang around with gay men
    D) A gay man who has the reputation of nagging others to get what he wants

262.   A "leather queen" is:

    A) A gay man whose apartment is exquisitely furnished with divine leather chairs
    B) A gay man who likes to wear leather and is attracted to men who enjoy wearing leather
    C) A gay man who grew up on a cattle ranch
    D) A gay man who has spent too much time in the sun and has skin as tough as cowhide

263. How is a woman referred to as a "bull-dyke" likely to be dressed?

    A) Well dressed in clothing that is very feminine,
       with pastel colors dominating her wardrobe
    B) Shirt: man's plaid work shirt; pants: jeans; shoes:
       black boots; makeup: none
    C) Silk dress with a string of pearls
    D) Gray flannel business suit with black high-heel
       shoes

264. Joe says that Harry really is a "maid of the mists." What does Joe mean?

    A) Harry *just loves* Niagara Falls.
    B) Harry adores his new at-home facial kit.
    C) Harry spends a lot of time at gay bathhouses.
    D) Harry is a true romantic and likes to walk in the
       rain.

265. Bill tells Carlos that "Mike was the best top man I have ever been with." What does Bill mean?

    A) Mike is great at being the active partner in their
       sex.
    B) Mike is great at tiling roofs.
    C) Mike is fabulous at icing cakes.
    D) Mike prefers riding on top of cars to riding inside
       them.

266. Nelly is one way of saying that a gay man is:

    A) Macho and deep voiced
    B) Very tall with extremely heavy musculature

C) Effeminate and affected in his mannerisms
D) New in town

267. Which of the following is *not* a Spanish word for homosexual?

A) *Maricon*
B) *Mariposa*
C) *Varon*
D) *Buey*

268. If someone says that a gay man is "butch," what is meant?

A) That he is very masculine, perhaps overmasculine
B) That he likes nicknames
C) That he likes to wear satin dresses when he is at home
D) That he is pretty in an effeminate way

269. Tom's brother Pete says that he wishes Tom would stop being such a fairy. What does Pete mean?

A) That he wishes Tom would act a little less masculine around women
B) That he really admires the way Tom always takes control of a situation, but he wishes Tom would give him a chance to handle some of their problems
C) "Tom, do you really have to act so queer?"
D) That he wishes Tom would be more careful with his money

270. Tom and Harry are on the phone "dishing" with each other. What does dishing mean?

A) That Tom and Harry are planning a dinner party
B) That Tom and Harry are involved in some vicious and delicious hot gossip
C) That Tom and Harry are talking to each other while they wash dirty dishes
D) That Tom and Harry are quizzing each other about which china pattern they want for their formal dinner parties

271. If someone says that a gay man "spent last night at the tubs," what does he mean?

A) That the gay man spent the last night bathing in order to get himself really clean for a great weekend
B) That the gay man spent an evening at a bathhouse
C) That the gay man spent an evening at a diet center discussing how to lose weight and rid himself of that tubby look
D) That the man had passsed the previous evening at a disco where there was a whirlpool in the middle of the dance floor

272. If a gay man says that he is going out cruising, what does he mean?

A) That he's going on a boat ride for a weekend
B) That he's going to drive his car until he finds a hill, go up the hill, then down the hill, and while doing so, put his car in neutral so it will cruise down the hill
C) That he's going to go out and look for a sexual partner

D) That he's taking his mother and her poodle to see
   the new Al Pacino movie

273. If a gay man says he is into S & M, what does he mean?

A) That he's into sex that involves singing and music
B) That he's into sex that involves sadism and mas-
   ochism
C) That he's into sales and money
D) That he's into sex and magic

274. If a gay man says that he has a fully equipped play-
room in his apartment, what does he mean?

A) That he has a swing set and slide in his apartment
B) That he has a stage where he acts out his child-
   hood fantasies
C) That he has a room equipped with leather, sexual
   toys, mirrors, and more for séxual experiences
D) That he has an at-home gymnasium

275. If a gay man says he wants to have "epidemic sex"
with you, what does he mean?

A) That he wants to have sex with you that would
   avoid the exchange of body fluids of any sort (also
   known as safe sex; some of the acts involved are
   mutual masturbation, hugging, and massage)
B) That he wants to have sex with you before the epidemic kills him
C) That he wants to have sex with you before he becomes infected by the epidemic
D) That he wants to have sex with you because he's
   afraid of the epidemic

276. Bill says to Tom, "I wish Pete wasn't such a disco queen." What does Bill mean?

  A) Bill wishes Pete weren't so afraid of going out dancing in the trendiest discos
  B) Bill wishes Pete didn't spend so much time at discos and had more time for him
  C) Bill wishes Pete would stop taking girls dancing at gay discos
  D) Bill wishes Pete would stop wearing dresses and tiaras when he goes to discos

10

FAMOUS HOMOSEXUALS AND BISEXUALS

The Book of Lists by David Wallechinsky, Irving Wallace, and Amy Wallace, using information from the *Advocate* (probably the most famous gay publication), lists the people in this chapter as some of the more notable homosexuals in history. The authors of *The Book of Lists* note that they only included those who had publicly disclosed their homosexuality.

How much do you know about the names that follow? Each question consists of a name and four biographical details. Your job is to distinguish which of the four facts does *not* describe the person.

277. Christina

   A) Swedish queen
   B) Discovered gravlax
   C) Born 1626
   D) Died 1689

278. Gertrude Stein

    A) Wrote plays, prose, and poetry
    B) Born in 1922
    C) Was Alice B. Toklas's lover
    D) Died in 1946

279. Bessie Smith

    A) First white woman to perform at the Cotton Club in Harlem
    B) Singer
    C) Born in the United States
    D) Died in 1937

280. Euripides

    A) Greek citizen
    B) Dramatist
    C) Born in A.D. 1122
    D) Died about 406 B.C.

281. Alexander the Great

    A) Macedonian ruler
    B) Close friend of Julius Caesar
    C) Born 356 B.C.
    D) Died 323 B.C.

282. Hadrian

    A) Citizen of Rome
    B) An emperor

C) Defeated Richard the Lion-Hearted during the
Battle of Vesuvius

D) Died at age sixty-two

283. Richard the Lion-Hearted

A) Born 1157
B) Died 1199
C) Citizen of Britain
D) A peasant whose life and adventures are now re-
told as the stories of Robin Hood

284. Sandro Botticelli

A) Greek citizen
B) Painter
C) Born approximately 1444
D) Died 1510

285. Leonardo da Vinci

A) Painter
B) Scientist/inventor
C) Italian
D) Born in 1565

286. Benvenuto Cellini

A) Goldsmith
B) Second cousin of Sandro Botticelli
C) Born in 1500
D) Died in 1571

287. Francis Bacon

    A) British citizen
    B) Philosopher
    C) Statesman
    D) Author of the Magna Carta

288. John Milton

    A) Blind
    B) Wrote *Paradise Lost*
    C) German citizen
    D) Died in 1674

289. Peter the Great

    A) Russian citizen
    B) A czar
    C) Born in 1672
    D) A paraplegic

290. Alexander von Humboldt

    A) American citizen
    B) Born in 1769
    C) Naturalist
    D) Died in 1859

291. Lord Byron

    A) Also known as Hans Bennett
    B) British citizen
    C) Poet
    D) Died in 1824

292.   Hans Christian Andersen

   A) Danish
   B) Sculptor
   C) Born in 1805
   D) Died in 1875

293.   Walt Whitman

   A) Wrote *The Waste Land*
   B) American
   C) Poet
   D) Died in 1892

294.   Pëtr Ilich Tchaikovsky

   A) Russian
   B) Playwright
   C) Born in 1840
   D) Died in 1893

295.   Paul Verlaine

   A) Chef
   B) Poet
   C) French
   D) Born in 1844

296.   Oscar Wilde

   A) Wrote *The Importance of Being Earnest*
   B) Born in 1826
   C) British
   D) Died in 1900

297.   Frederick Rolfe

    A) Also known as Baron Corvo
    B) Italian
    C) Author
    D) Died at age fifty-three

298.   Marcel Proust

    A) Wrote *Remembrance of Things Past*
    B) Playwright
    C) French citizen
    D) Died in 1922

299.   E. M. Forster

    A) British citizen
    B) Wrote *Maurice*
    C) Wrote *Far from the Madding Crowd*
    D) Died in 1970

300.   John Maynard Keynes

    A) American citizen
    B) Economist
    C) Lytton Strachey's lover
    D) Died in 1946

301.   T. E. Lawrence

    A) Immortalized in the movie *Dr. Zhivago*
    B) Author
    C) British citizen
    D) Soldier

302. Bill Tilden

    A) Tennis player
    B) Known as Big Bill
    C) Transsexual
    D) Died at age seventy

303. Christopher Isherwood

    A) British citizen
    B) Wrote *A Single Man*
    C) Born in London
    D) Wrote *Christopher and His Kind*

304. Dag Hammarskjöld

    A) Swedish
    B) United Nations secretary general
    C) Died in 1961
    D) Founded Haagen Dazs ice cream company

305. W. H. Auden

    A) Wrote a poem called "The Platonic Blow"
    B) Born in York, England
    C) German citizen
    D) Died in 1982

306. Jean Genet

    A) French citizen
    B) Playwright
    C) Wrote *The Balcony*
    D) Born in 1926

307. Tennessee Williams

    A) Playwright
    B) Wrote *Cat on a Hot Tin Roof*
    C) Born in 1911
    D) Wrote *Travels with My Aunt*

308. Pier Paolo Pasolini

    A) Filmmaker
    B) Directed *Salo*
    C) Was murdered
    D) Directed *Il Posto*

309. Allen Ginsberg

    A) Poet
    B) Born in 1942
    C) Birthplace: Brooklyn, New York
    D) Part of the "beat" school

ANSWERS

1. **B)** When the "beat" poet of the fifties and sixties
    went to Oxford to visit Auden (who reportedly
    couldn't stand Ginsberg's poetry), the young man
    shocked his host by kneeling and—in complete sincer-
    ity—kissing his trouser cuffs.

2. **A)** *The Blind Bow-Boy.* A randy duke had stationery
    emblazoned with the motto.

3. **C)** King James I. Born in 1566, he followed in his gay
    father's footsteps when it came to his sexual inclina-
    tions, but was unable to act on them. However, within
    royal circles, James's leanings were as well known as
    his father's. One joke had it, "We have had King Eliza-
    beth, now we have Queen James."

4. **C)** Though at least one of the other names listed had
    affairs with women, it was Judy Holliday.

5. **A)** Marilyn Monroe

6. **C)** Vaslav Nijinsky was Diaghilev's lover, then his choreographer.

7. **B)** A pioneer in the Off-Off Broadway movement, Doric Wilson is completely committed to alternative theater.

8. **B)** Jack Wrangler

9. **C)** Henri III was reputed to be so effeminate that he would run, shrieking like a girl, downstairs to hide in the cellars during thunderstorms.

10. **B)** Pavel Tchelitchew

11. **A) and C)** Augustus Caesar was born Caius Octavius and was called Octavius before becoming emperor.

12. **A)** Lady Una Trowbridge

13. **A)** Lorenz Hart

14. **D)** May Sarton

15. **B)** Rudolph Valentino

16. **D)** The others, all her lovers, were, respectively, an actress, a poet, and an English actress.

17. **B) and C)** Sand is Amandine Dupin's pseudonym.

18. **A)** Although all listed are known to be gay, it is only Capote who was born in New Orleans.

19. **C)** Mauritz Stiller

20. **D)** David Bowie told *Playboy* in 1976 that he was bi-sexual, as was his wife, whom he met when they were both going out with the same man.

21. True. Mineo said that after leaving a seance at which he had been trying to contact James Dean, he was in a car crash, but miraculously his life was spared, and the name "James Dean" appeared on the wrecked car's windshield. From that moment on Mineo claimed he was gay.

22. **D)** Edward Perry Warren

23. **C)** An autopsy revealed traces of amyl nitrate in the body of Paul Lynde (who will forever be remembered for his campy humor on the television game show "Hollywood Squares"), which leads one to certain conclusions about what he may have been doing just before his death.

24. **B)** Baron Friedrich von Steuben was made inspector general of the United States by the Continental Congress, and after Steuben went through his own personal fortune aiding the United States Army, Congress repaid him with a pension and land, which he left in his will to two handsome young soldiers whom he'd "adopted."

25. **A)** Martin Gaye

26. **B)** Brooke's beauty is said to have prompted Lytton Strachey and John Maynard Keynes to fight over the privilege of wooing him while they were at Cambridge.

27. **A)** Both of these Richards were known to be gay.

28. **D)** Christina, who lived from 1626 to 1689

29. **C)** Merle Miller

30. **A)** Paul Verlaine

31. **C)** Constance Lloyd

32. **D)** Cyril and Vivyan

33. **C)** And until her death in 1969, Erika Mann remained the wife of W. H. Auden, even though theirs was solely a platonic relationship.

34. **B)** We say "thought," because Dag Hammarskjöld's biographer claims otherwise—even though during Hammarskjöld's tenure at the United Nations it was strongly felt by many in the diplomatic community that he was. The fact that he never married, loved gourmet food and fresh flowers means not a thing in our consideration.

35. **C)** His lover beat him to death with a hammer, then killed himself.

36. **A)** Heckler also announced on this date that a new process had been developed to mass-produce the probable AIDS-causing virus—an essential step toward understanding the nature of the virus.

37. **D)** HTLV-3 is a human retrovirus related to the HTLV (Human T-Lymphotropic virus) family and to the retrovirus, discovered over a year ago by French

researchers, who called it LAV (Lymphadenopathy-
Associated Virus).

38. **A)** The Gay Pride Run

39. **C)** David Kopay

40. **A)** Running back

41. **D)** The Forty-Niners, Lions, and Redskins

42. **A)** Christopher Street Book Shop

43. **D)** Everard Bath

44. **A)** Patrick Cowley

45. **C)** Dr. James Curran

46. True, according to the American Liver Foundation
     and the Center for Disease Control in Atlanta, Georgia

47. False. There is a GAA, but its central office is based in
     Los Angeles. They may be contacted by writing: Gay
     Alcoholics Anonymous, 1322 North Van Ness Avenue,
     Los Angeles, CA 90028.

48. **A)** Or more commonly known as venereal warts

49. **C)** Ethyl chloride

50. **A)** and **D)** The Pines and Cherry Grove

51. **B**

52. **D)** The shamans, catamites and Indians

53. True

54. **A)** Bill Tilden

55. **A)** There were six Village People: Indian, construction worker, sailor, soldier, cowboy, and leather queen.

56. True

57. False. Almost all require that you sign on as a "member" and pay an admission fee. For this, you usually get a towel and a room.

58. **B)** Glory-holes

59. **D)** If you want to get into the Mine Shaft, don't wear cologne, designer clothes, or a striped shirt.

60. True

61. **D)** Golden showers and water sports

62. **D)** The Meat Rack

63. False. The only way to get to the Pines is by ferry, private boat, or seaplane.

64. False. On the contrary, Fire Island, especially the Pines, is for some prohibitively expensive—particularly the summer house rentals, which can run up to $18,000 per season, though the average is $3,000 to $5,000. It is definitely a resort community for the upscale gay.

65. **C)** Martina Navratilova

66. **B)** Tearooms

67. **D**

68. **B)** Ball spreader

69. False. In most big cities, having sex (especially mutual masturbation and oral sex) while the movie is playing is expected.

70. **C)** Scott Thorson filed the suit, which was later dismissed.

71. True. New York/New Jersey Governor Cornbury (1702–1709) often appeared in drag at both official and unofficial functions, a fact quite often overlooked in official histories of the state. One wonders, though, what dress size the governor was.

72. **A)** According to Vern Bullough's *Homosexuality: A History,* the first reported trial took place in 1631, during the reign of King Charles I. The case involved the earl of Castlehaven who was charged with sodomizing one of his male servants, raping his own wife, then sodomizing her too. Not exactly shy, was he? The verdict was guilty, fifteen to twelve, and the earl was executed on May 14, 1631.

73. **D)** Wilde went through three trials, the first of which was a libel suit he himself initiated against the father of Lord Alfred Douglas (with whom he'd been having an affair) after Douglas's father called him a "sodomite." He eventually withdrew the charges when it began to look as though Douglas's father had enough

evidence to prove Wilde's homosexuality. Nonetheless, on the basis of the evidence gathered, Wilde was tried under the terms of the amended criminal laws enacted by Henry Labouchere, a member of Parliament. It was a hung jury in the second trial, but Wilde was tried again, found guilty of acts of gross indecency, and sentenced to two years at hard labor. All in all, Wilde suffered through three trials and two years of hard labor.

74. **D)** The key law on the subject prescribes the death penalty for anal intercourse. According to historians, this law, set forth in A.D. 390 by Roman emperors Theodosius I, Valentinian II, and Arcadius, has had the most influence on modern Western attitudes. The law reads: "All persons who have the shameful custom of condemning a man's body, acting the part of a woman's, to the sufferance of an alien sex (for they appear not to be different from women), shall expiate a crime of this kind by avenging flames in the sight of the people."

75. True. Plato was the lover of Alexis of Dion, and Aristotle was the lover of his pupil Hermias. Euripides, the playwright, was the lover of the poet Agathon.

76. True. In those days, the lover was expected to declare his love openly, and homosexual love was linked with valor and courage and said to have been justified by the gods. It is said Plato himself believed that the strongest armies in the world would be ones where lovers were linked together, inspiring each other to deeds of heroism and sacrifice. In fact, there was an army called the Sacred Band of the Thebes, which consisted primarily of about three hundred men

grouped as pairs of lovers who were responsible for the brief period of military supremacy of Thebes.

77. **B)** In 1897, The Wissenschaftlich-humanitare Kommittee (Scientific Humanitarian Committee) was formed by Magnus Hirschfeld, probably the first public gay activist. The committee's purpose was to carry out research and lobby for change in the Prussian and German laws on homosexuality, and in 1899 they published a journal, *Jahrbuch fur sexuelle Zwischenstufen*, which is generally regarded as the first public journal of homosexual studies.

78. **C)** The first organization of lesbians was the Daughters of Bilitis (so named from a poem by Pierre Louys entitled "Songs of Bilitis") and was founded by Phyllis Lyon, a lesbian activist, and six other women.

79. **B)** 1955

80. **B)** The postmaster of Los Angeles withdrew the October 1954 issue and One, Inc. went to court. In 1955, the U.S. District Court in southern California decided that the magazine was nonmailable, since the "stories are obviously calculated to stimulate the lust of the homosexual reader." The decision was later appealed, then sustained, and in 1958, One, Inc. went before the Supreme Court and won. This was considered perhaps the first significant Supreme Court victory by the increasingly vocal homosexual community.

81. **D)** The variety store clerk was the prototype of today's hairdressers, florists, and interior decorators. They were called "counter jumpers" because, it was

said, they would leap over the counters to wait on attractive male customers.

82. **C)** Frederick the Great, king of Prussia from 1740 to 1786, was forced to watch the decapitation of his lover, Hans von Katte, by order of Frederick's father, Frederick William, who had been appalled by his heir's blatant love affair with Katte. Just before Katte was decapitated, however, the young Frederick blew him a kiss and begged forgiveness. Then he fainted and was spared seeing the actual decapitation.

83. **D)** Homophile was used because the suffix -*phile* was supposed to suggest that homosexuality was more an emotion than a sexual attraction and that homosexuals were interested in love more than sex, just like heterosexuals.

84. **B)** *The Homosexual in America* by Donald Webster Cory was published in 1951 by Greenberg Publishers, the only company willing to handle such controversial material. The book was the first to encourage homosexuals in America to fight for their civil rights.

85. **A)** On June 27, 1969, eight police officers tried to close down the Stonewall Inn, but when a police van arrived to take suspects to precinct headquarters, a melée of bottle heaving, the stoning of police officers, and the throwing of fire bombs ensued. The police barricaded themselves inside the Stonewall, but the crowds outside uprooted a parking meter and used it as a battering ram on the Stonewall door. It took several more police cars—and almost thirty riot-control policemen—to get things under control. But it marked the first time that homosexuals fought harassment in numbers, and the Gay Liberation Movement was born.

86. **A)** *Lesbos* is considered one of the earliest lesbian-
     oriented magazines, and was published in the 1930s by
     a Dutch group associated with gay activist Magnus
     Hirschfeld.

87. **A)** The APA voted in April 1974 to remove homosex-
     uality from its list of mental disorders after its board of
     trustees had decided to do so the previous December
     and place the matter before the association's members.

88. **B)** The Mattachine Foundation was formed on April
     Fools' Day, 1950. Its name came from the medieval
     jesters who spoke the truth to authoritarian rulers. Ac-
     cording to Vern Bullough's *Homosexuality: A History,*
     in the early days the Mattachine Foundation was simi-
     lar to Alcoholics Anonymous, since secrecy was a by-
     word and its chief purpose was to help its members
     live well-oriented and socially productive lives.

89. **B)** In 1945 a group of New York City Quakers asked
     New York City psychiatrist George W. Henry to head
     up the Quaker Emergency Committee, which was de-
     dicated to assisting gays in conflict with the law.

90. **A)** The Knights of the Clock

91. **D)** Student Homophile League

92. **C)** Columbia

93. **A)** April 1967

94. **C)** Randolphe Wicker, a successful businessman, was
     the first gay to speak as a homosexual on radio. This
     occurred in New York in 1962.

116

95. **D)** *Life*

96. **A)** 1964

97. **B)** Jimmy Walker

98. **B)** The term *gay* entered the American lexicon right after World War I. During the twenties it became widely used among gays to describe themselves, but it did not reach outside circles until the forties.

99. **C)** The forties. (Goldman died in 1940.)

100. **A)** "Aunt Wheeler"

101. **A)** October 1962, by Franklin Kameny, a key figure in the history of gay liberation and founder of the Mattachine Society of Washington, D.C.

102. **C)** Lorena Hickock. It has been strenuously denied that Hickock and Eleanor Roosevelt had a lesbian relationship, but it has been proven that Hickock herself was a lesbian and had numerous lesbian affairs. (Read Doris Faber's *Lorena: The Life of Lorena Hickock.*)

103. **C)** Maclean and Burgess were two spies who, because of their homosexuality, gave new meaning to the term "security risk."

104. **C)** "Lisa Ben" was the pseudonym.

105. **A)** 1970

106. **C)** He had sex with three parishioners and a mare. The clergyman was the Rev. John Wilson.

107. **D)** Although there is no concrete proof, these words are attributed to the great poet, who was born in 1564 and died in 1593.

108. **D)** Saladin was known to have kept a large stable of boys and/or eunuchs during his reign.

109. **B)** The *pedicon* has anal intercourse with the *cinede*.

110. **B)** Caesar

111. **B)** *The Thousand and One Nights*

112. **C)** Alfred Kinsey, in his *Sexual Behavior in the Human Male*

113. **A)** Apparently, the Celts were not alone. If historians are correct, male gayness was common in all Europe, even before the advent of Christianity.

114. **C)** *The Gay Brothers* was an experimental sound film directed by William Dickson for the Thomas Edison Studio.

115. **B)** The two gay men were played by Farley Granger and John Dall.

116. **D)** *The Children's Hour,* with Shirley MacLaine and Audrey Hepburn, was based on the Lillian Hellman play.

117. **C)** Barbara Stanwyck, in a little-known but unforgettable role

118. **A)** From Jean Genet's play of the same name

119.   **C)** *Partners* was a terribly unfunny attempt to cash in on the success of *La Cage aux Folles*.

120.   **C)** *The Best Man*

121.   **C)** Fred Zinnemann, *The Day of the Jackal*

122.   **B)** Dirk Bogarde played Aschenbach. Aschenbach's sexual preferences are never made explicit, although many readers of Thomas Mann's novella insist that he is a gay man.

123.   **C)** Al Pacino plays the cop whose own sexual identity crisis becomes the focal point of *Cruising*.

124.   **D)** *Barbarella,* a film that Jane Fonda would surely love to forget she ever made

125.   **C)** *The Kremlin Letter,* John Huston's version of Noel Behn's best-selling book

126.   **C)** Wint and Kidd were the two gay lovers whose favorite sport was murder.

127.   **B)** A hatpin in the neck does Gorman's character in.

128.   **D)** *Play It as It Lays* is based on Joan Didion's novel of the same name.

129.   **C)** *Saint Jack*

130.   **A)** *The Third Sex,* directed by Frank Winterstein

131.   **B)** Paul Newman directed and received much praise for *Rachel, Rachel,* which starred Newman's wife, Joanne Woodward.

132. **D)** *Gay News*

133. **C)** *Bloodbrothers*

134. **B)** *The Boys in the Band.* The successful movie was based on Mart Crowley's ground-breaking play.

135. **C)** *Sunday, Bloody Sunday.* The homosexual doctor was played by the late Peter Finch, the heterosexual career woman by Glenda Jackson, and the bisexual artist by Murry Head.

136. **B)** *Dog Day Afternoon.* Directed by Sidney Lumet, *Dog Day Afternoon* was based on a true story.

137. **D)** *La Dolce Vita,* directed by the great Italian film director Federico Fellini

138. **A)** Robert Altman is one of very few filmmakers who would dare to show lesbians as well adjusted and happy.

139. **B)** *Car Wash.* Lindy was played by character actor Antonio Fargas.

140. **C)** *Butley.* Directed by playwright Harold Pinter, *Butley* was based on Simon Gray's play of the same name.

141. **D)** *California Suite,* based on Neil Simon's Broadway play of the same name.

142. **A)** *Fame,* directed by Alan Parker. More unusual than the fact that an openly gay character was included in this commercial film was the fact that he seemed to be

the only gay in the High School of the Performing Arts, and all of New York, for that matter.

143.   **C)** *Exodus*

144.   **D)** June Allyson. To play the part of the lesbian, Allyson was told to show up on the set dressed as a lesbian would. She arrived wearing her son's football jersey. The perfect lesbian!

145.   **D)** *American Gigolo.* Directed by Paul Schrader, *American Gigolo* features an unsavory and stereotypical cast of gay characters: a lesbian pimp, a black pimp, a murderer, and a closet case who hates women and likes to watch his wife get beaten up.

146.   **A)** Rod Steiger. Directed by Tony Richardson, *The Loved One* is a wonderful, often forgotten black comedy, which is, unfortunately, loaded with stereotypical gay characters.

147.   True. The word *homosexual* was not used until the nineteenth century.

148.   True. There are numerous references to relations between men that have been interpreted as homosexual, but there is little if any mention of lesbianism. (See *Sex Laws and Customs in Judaism* by Louis M. Epstein [New York: Bloch, 1948.])

149.   **A)** The MCC was founded on October 6, 1968, in Los Angeles, California.

150.   **C)** *The Lord Is My Shepherd and He Knows I'm Gay*

151.   **A)** The MCC's theology

152.   **D)** *In Unity: The Gay Christian*

153.   **B)** Chaim Chaham Chadashim

154.   True. In fact, Martin Luther wrote, "The heinous con-
duct of the people of Sodom is extraordinary, inas-
much as they departed from the natural passion and
longing of the male for the female, which was im-
planted by God, and desired what is altogether contrary to nature. Whence comes this perversity?
Undoubtedly from Satan." Although Protestant theo-
logian John Calvin didn't go this far, he was against
homosexuality or any other form of intercourse that
didn't lead to procreation.

155.   **A)** Leviticus 18:22, which reads, "Thou shalt not lie
with mankind as with womankind: it is an abomination." And Leviticus 21:13 goes on, "If a man also lie
with mankind, as he lieth with a woman, both of them
have committed an abomination: they shall surely be
put to death; and their blood shall be upon them."

156.   True. Biblical scholar Derrick Sherwin Bailey has evidence to support this, and he says that in the original
Scriptures, the antihomosexual aspects of the men
wanting "to know" Lot's guests did not exist.

157.   True. More important, none of the biblical references
to Sodom explains exactly what crimes the residents
were guilty of—beyond that of pride, unwillingness to
aid the poor and needy, haughtiness, and the doing of
abominable things—all of which many other biblical
peoples and cities have demonstrated.

158.   True. Jesus actually said very little about sex, except as
        it pertained to divorce and remarriage, which he for-
        bade. However, though Jesus himself doesn't say any-
        thing about homosexuality, epistle writers did, and
        quite explicitly. For example, see 1 Corinthians
        6:9–10.

159.   C) Donna Summer

160.   C) Jerry Falwell said this in his book *Listen, America!*
        (New York: Doubleday, 1980).

161.   D) Ezra, Sahl, and Ghayyath

162.   True

163.   D) In the Old Testament, Saul and David, David and
        Jonathan, and Ruth and Naomi were all noted for their
        mutual love. They were celebrated through the Mid-
        dle Ages in both ecclesiastical and popular literature
        as examples of extraordinary devotion.

164.   C) David says this to Jonathan in 2 Samuel 1:26.

165.   D) Most conservative interpretations have agreed that
        there are twelve specific references to gay people in
        the Bible.

166.   A) In direct response to Peter Cantor's urging, the
        first ecumenical council ruling on homosexual acts was
        Latern III of 1179. Reacting to growing European in-
        tolerance of all forms of nonconformity, the council
        imposed sanctions against moneylenders, heretics,
        Jews, Muslims, mercenaries. Homosexuals were to be
        excommunicated, and members of the clergy who

committed homosexual acts were deposed from office
or confined to a monastery. This passed into the per-
manent collections of canon law, compiled in the thir-
teenth century.

167. False. Surprisingly, usury, not adultery, incurred more
      severe penalties in church law than did sodomy.

168. **A)** Both were monks in his order. Simon, until his
      death, was the mainstay of Aelred's life. Afterward
      Aelred was heartbroken and said that he did not want
      to continue living.

169. **D)** Richard the Lion-Hearted

170. **B)** Bourgueil was known for his openly homoerotic
      poetry. As bishop, he had a lover named Peter whose
      comb he carried with him at all times as a memento of
      their love.

171. **B)** Perhaps the most thoroughly researched reassess-
      ment of the Bible's views on homosexuality, this book
      was written by John Boswell, an assistant professor of
      history at Yale University and was published in 1980
      by the Chicago University Press.

172. **A)** Glide Memorial Church

173. **B)** 1978

174. **A)** 1978

175. **D)** Unitarians and Catholics

176. **D)** Onan

177. **B)** For information, write: *Forum*, Box 891, Oak Park,
      IL 60303.

178. **A**

179. False. The American Baptist Gay Caucus is based in
      Philadelphia, Pennsylvania.

180. False. There is a religion committee in the National
      Gay Task Force.

181. **D)** This task force is based in Miami, Florida.

182. **C)** On their last album, *The Hunter*, Blondie included
      a song by Debbie Harry about a person who, it is im-
      plied, is gay.

183. **D)** Antonina Ivanovna Miliukova married Pëtr Ilich
      Tchaikovsky, even though she knew of his preference
      for men. The marriage was never consummated.
      (Tchaikovsky also had an unhealthy devotion to the
      memory of his mother, who had died when he was
      fourteen.

184. **A)** Marcel Proust

185. **D)** *Silk Electric*

186. **B)** "Do You Really Want to Hurt Me?"

187. **B)** Bessie Smith, who was a lover of another blues
      singer, Ma Rainey

188. **C)** Poulenc

189.   False. According to Martin Grief in *The Gay Book of Days*, Bowie used to perform mock blow jobs on his guitarist Mike Ronson.

190.   **C)** Joplin, according to Myra Friedman in *Buried Alive*, though the author contends her exploits were exaggerated

191.   False. It isn't even known whether Handel in fact *was* gay, though historians speculate he probably was. What is known is that he was celibate for most of his life.

192.   **C)** Marc Blitzstein

193.   **C)** A hustler

194.   **B)** Wanda Landowska

195.   **A)** Henry Cowell

196.   **D)** *Rolling Stone*

197.   **A)** "Modern Love." The lyrics go: "I catch the paper boy/but things don't really change."

198.   True

199.   **B)** Saint-Saëns

200.   **C)** Divine

201.   **B)** *Jungle Jezebel*

202.   **C)** and **D)** Carson McCullers married Reeves
       McCullers, who was gay and who eventually had an
       affair with composer David Diamond, with whom
       McCullers herself was involved.

203.   **A)** Bowen's novel is about the friendship between a
       young woman and a middle-aged widow. Later in life,
       the novelist is quoted as saying she could find nothing
       unnatural about the love between women.

204.   **C)** According to Charles Osborne, Auden's biogra-
       pher, Auden publicly challenged Gide, saying, "He's a
       conceited liar. How could he have an orgasm after a
       night of fucking? I'll bet he couldn't even produce an
       erection."

205.   **C)** *Dreams Die First* (New York: Simon & Schuster,
       1977) is a roman à clef about a down-and-out magazine
       publisher who turns to publishing porn, and his dalli-
       ances along the road to fame with men and women.

206.   True. In a *People* magazine interview in 1977, Robbins
       claims to have "experimented" with bisexuality in his
       research for *Dreams Die First.*

207.   **C)** Gerald Haxton was Maugham's live-in lover for
       many years. Among those who became very close to
       both men was Robin Maugham, Somerset's nephew,
       who was also gay and a novelist. He wrote, among
       others, *The Servant.*

208.   **C)** *South Wind* tells, in part, the story of how this
       Scottish novelist decided to leave his wife and settle on
       the island of Capri, where he felt free to lead a homo-
       sexual life-style.

209. **A)** Graves's only known work about homosexuality is the play *But It Still Goes On.*

210. True. Auden wrote "The Platonic Blow" in 1948 for his own amusement. *Fuck You: A Magazine of the Arts* published the poem without his permission in 1965, which led to the publication of three hundred copies of a "trade edition" and a "rough trade" edition of five copies, each of which included "beautiful slurp drawings by the artist Joe Brainard." Auden admitted authorship of the poem in 1968.

211. **B)** Susan Sontag wrote "Notes on 'Camp' " in 1964, in which she offers the definitive explanation of camp. Some of the examples of camp that Sontag listed are:

   Tiffany lamps
   The Brown Derby restaurant on Sunset Boulevard in Los Angeles
   The Enquirer, headlines and stories
   Shoedsack's *King Kong*
   Swan Lake
   Stag movies seen without lust

212. **A)** Clem Snide the Private Asshole is the only one of the four characters listed who has appeared in previous Burroughs novels. Snide is a private asshole (detective) on the trail of a kid who's been missing for two months. Looking at his photo, Snide says, "Jerry was a beautiful kid. Slender, red hair, green eyes far apart, a wide mouth, sexy and kinky-looking." Jerry, as we find out, is gay, as is Clem Snide the Private Asshole.

213. **B)** Maugham lived in Villa Mauresque, on the Riviera, surrounded by a wall bearing a Moorish symbol that became his trademark. The villa housed an exten-

sive art collection, including several Picassos, and was furnished in a Spanish baroque style. It is now owned by oil and gas billionaire Oscar Wyatt and his socialite wife, Lynne.

214. **D)** Ned Rorem authored *The Paris Diary* and the subsequent *New York Diary* (1967), both of which cover various aspects of his own homosexuality, and both of which became major literary events upon publication. His music has been performed by Leonard Bernstein, Leontyne Price, Eugene Ormandy, Leopold Stowkowski, and many others. He is also the author of *Setting the Tone* (New York: Coward-McCann, 1983), a collection of essays and a diary.

215. **A)** Chicago

216. **C)** *The Hand That Cradles the Rock* (1974) was the first book published by Rita Mae Brown.

217. **B)** *How to Save Your Own Life* (New York: Holt, Rinehart & Winston, 1977)

218. **C)** Rosanna Howard

219. **B)** Jong writes: "Finally, finally, after a month of bottles, vibrators, fruit, and pulsating water, I had the pleasure of seeing Rosanna Howard reach tumultuous orgasm with the bulging green base of a Dom Perignon bottle protruding from her reluctant cunt."

220. **A)** *Compulsion* by Meyer Levin, though a roman à clef about the Leopold and Loeb murder of Bobby Franks, is drenched in Freudian overtones. Judd Steiner and Artie Strauss are thinly disguised versions

of Leopold and Loeb, and Levin describes the men as having a relationship that is clearly homosexual. At one point Judd even refers to himself as a "cocksucker."

221. **A) and B)** President Joe Prescott, who heads Prescott College in upstate New York, where Warren's novel takes place, is both aware of and accepting of Brown's homosexuality. And, as we discover, Billy Sive and Brown fall in love.

222. **D)** *Consenting Adults* was published in 1975 and deals with a seventeen-year-old boy telling his family he is gay, his therapy and try and change his feelings, the therapy's lack of success, and ultimately, the boy's—and the family's—acceptance of his homosexuality.

223. **D)** *Dress Grey* by Lucian Truscott IV was published in 1979 to a great deal of controversy, not only because of its subject matter, but because Truscott himself had once been a plebe at West Point.

224. **C)** Malone was the name of the young man who, having left behind a law firm on Wall Street, pursued Manhattan and Fire Island's gay life for nearly ten years before disappearing into the ocean one summer.

225. True. Hansen and his wife, Jane, recently celebrated their fortieth wedding anniversary.

226. **A and B**

227. **C)** White's "First Love" appeared in *Christopher Street* magazine and was then reprinted in the fine volume *Aphrodisiac: Fiction from Christopher Street* (New York: Coward-McCann & Geoghegan, 1980).

228. **C)** Referring to the United States' views on homosexuality, Gore Vidal said this in an interview in *Oui* in 1975.

229. **D)** In *Music for Chameleons* (New York: Random House, 1980), Truman Capote wrote those words in a late-night interview with himself.

230. **A)** *The End of My Life* by Vance Bourjailly explored homosexual behavior and the search for a meaningful life. It was important because it included ideas about the cause of homosexuality, which were popular at the time.

231. **D)** *Advise and Consent* was published by Doubleday in 1959 to immediate success and controversy. The novel revolves around the Senate confirmation of a Secretary of State and one of the men of great conscience in the Congress, Senator Brigham Anderson of Utah, who opposes the nominee. Anderson, however, is susceptible to blackmail because he had a homosexual affair with a man while he was in the military. When it begins to look as though this affair may come to light, Anderson commits suicide, tragically ending a fine career and a valuable life.

232. **A)** *The Book of Ebenezer Le Page* by G. B. Edwards, with an introduction by John Fowles, was published to great critical acclaim in March 1981 by Alfred A. Knopf.

233. **D)** *Bent* by Martin Sherman

234. **B)** Although there are references to gayness or minor gay characters in previous plays, Marlowe's is the first play extant with a homosexual as its main character.

235.   **C)** Fierstein, in addition to winning a Tony as best playwright, won the Tony award for best actor in a play for his performance in *Torch Song Trilogy*.

236.   **D)** The puns are light references and not direct recognitions of a character's homosexuality or heterosexuality.

237.   **B)** *Last Summer at Bluefish Cove*

238.   **A)** *Sodom: Or, the Quintessence of Debauchery*

239.   **B)** *La Cage Aux Folles*, with Gene Barry and George Hearn

240.   **C)** *The Drag* never made it to the Broadway stage. According to William M. Hoffman, author of *Gay Plays: The First Collection*, only two copies of *The Drag* exist, one with Ms. West's estate; the other—minus a page—in the Library of Congress.

241.   **A)** Wilde, surprisingly, never wrote a gay play. Although references to gayness abound in Wilde's work, no overtly gay play would have been allowed on the stage in his era.

242.   **C)** *Troilus and Cressida, As You Like It,* and *Twelfth Night,* as well as *Antony and Cleopatra,* include many references to homosexuality. Also, in many of Shakespeare's "romantic" comedies, where there is much transvestism, there is an element of implied or denied homosexuality.

243.   **C**

244. **C)** In *A Chorus Line* Paul is gay; in *T-Shirts* all the characters are gay; in *A Taste of Honey* Geoffrey is gay.

245. **B)** *Entertaining Mr. Sloane*

246. **C)** *On Golden Pond*

247. **C)** Robert Graves

248. **D)** *The Ritz*

249. **D)** *Night of the Iguana*

250. **A)** *The Children's Hour*

251. **B)** *Fortune and Men's Eyes*

252. **D)** Harry Kondoleon

253. **A)** *The Fifth of July*

254. **D**

255. **B**

256. **D**

257. **B**

258. **C**

259. **A**

260. **A**

261. **C**

262. **B**

263. **B**

264. **C**

265. **A**

266. **C**

267. **C**

268. **A**

269. **C**

270. **B**

271. **B**

272. **C**

273. **B**

274. **C**

275. **A**

276. **B**

277. **B)** Christina did not discover gravlax.

278. **B)** Gertrude Stein was actually born in 1874 and died in 1946.

279. **A)** Bessie Smith was one of the great blues singers of all time. She also happened to be a black woman.

280. **C)** Euripides was long dead in 1122. His approximate date of birth is 480 B.C.

281. **B)** To be a close friend of Julius Caesar, Alexander the Great would have had to live to be at least 256 years old. Julius Caesar was not born until 100 B.C. Alexander the Great was born in 356 B.C.

282. **B)** Since there was no Battle of Vesuvius it would have been hard to defeat someone during it. Even more difficult would be going to war with someone who wasn't born until you were nearly 1000 years old.

283. **D)** Although Richard the Lion-Hearted may have been, or may not have been, of peasant stock, he certainly was king of England. He was not the basis for the character now known as Robin Hood.

284. **A)** Botticelli was an Italian citizen.

285. **D)** Da Vinci was born in 1452.

286. **B)** Cellini was not related to Botticelli.

287. **D)** Although his accomplishments were many, Bacon did not write the Magna Carta.

288. **C)** Milton was British.

289. **D)** Peter the Great was not paraplegic.

290. **A)** Von Humboldt was German.

291. **A)** Lord Byron was also known as George Gordon.

292. **B)** Andersen was an author.

293. **A)** Eliot wrote *The Waste Land.* Whitman is best known for *Leaves of Grass.*

294. **B)** Tchaikovsky was a composer.

295. **A)** Verlaine was not a chef by profession.

296. **B)** Wilde was born in 1854.

297. **B)** Rolfe was British not Italian.

298. **B)** Proust was a writer, but of prose, not plays.

299. **C)** Thomas Hardy wrote *Far from the Madding Crowd.*

300. **A)** Keynes was British.

301. **A)** Lawrence was immortalized in David Lean's *Lawrence of Arabia,* a film that recounted some of Lawrence's experiences in the Near East.

302. **C)** Tilden was not a transsexual.

303. **C)** Isherwood was not born in London, but in High Lane, near Stockport, Cheshire.

304. **D)** Hammarskjöld did not found an ice cream company.

305. **C)** Auden had dual British–U.S. citizenship.

306. **D)** Genet was born in 1910.

307. **D)** Patrick Dennis wrote *Travels with My Aunt*.

308. **D)** Ermano Olmi directed *Il Posto*.

309. **C)** Ginsberg was born in Paterson, New Jersey.